Collected Verse 2001-2021

Previous Poetry Publications
(published by Crowlin Press unless otherwise stated)
Kindly Clouds
The Bountiful Loch
the saga of fnc gull
An Altitude Within *(Kennedy & Boyd)*
Redomones *(Kennedy & Boyd)*
Riding to Trapalanda
Walking to the Island
Sonnets to Hugh MacDiarmid, and Other Scots Poems

Other Publications
Teaching Scottish Literature *(editor) (Edinburgh University Press)*
R.B. Cunninghame Graham: Collected Stories and Sketches (in five volumes) *(joint editor) (Kennedy & Boyd)*

Collected Verse

2001-2021

Alan MacGillivray

Published by
Kennedy & Boyd
an imprint of
Zeticula Ltd
Unit 13
196 Rose Street
Edinburgh
EH2 4AT
Scotland

http://www.kennedyandboyd.co.uk
admin@kennedyandboyd.co.uk

An Altitude Within first published in 2010
the saga of fnc gull first published 2009
Redomones, and Eye to the Future first published in 2016
Riding to Trapalanda first published in 2018
Walking to the Island (with Insular Poems) first published in 2018
Sonnets to Hugh MacDiarmid, and Other Scots Poems first
published in 2020
On the Banks of Nith and *Laughing at Confucius* have not been
previously published.

First published in this format 2022

ISBN 978-1-84921-132-1 hardback
ISBN 978-1-84921-133-8 paperback

To Isobel

Acknowledgements

I wish to thank all the following for their help and inspiration over the years of writing these verses.

Donny O'Rourke
John C. McIntyre
John Gair
Brian Smith
Robbie Schneider
Robin Cunninghame Graham
Janie and Francis Minay

Ronald Renton
Stuart Johnston
Denise Joy Carruthers
Andrew Sandison
Marcia Dominguez Nisbet
Dai Vaughan
Catriona MacGillivray

Lesley Duncan and the organisers of the James McCash Scots Poetry Competition

Duncan Jones and the Association for Scottish Literature

Joseph Farrell and the Cunninghame Graham Society

An anonymous Brighton sea-gull

My dear wife, Isobel MacGillivray

Contents

Acknowledgements   *vii*

An Altitude Within   1

   Black and White   2

   A Seasonal Catalogue   3

   for ever   4

   Night-Town   6

   Forebodings   7

   Character   8

   The Selkie and the Drunks   9

   A New Kind of Hero   10

   From the Gaelic   11

   Carranaich   12

   Crowlin Mor   13

   Torridons   14

   Cathair   15

   Uniforms   16

   Sonnet   17

   The Owl and the Pussycat   18

   Reid   19

   Lunar Eclipse   20

   from Two Native Lands — A Love Song   21

   Departing   22

   Flower Power   23

   Signs of the Day   24

   Coming Ashore   25

   The Interlude   26

   Lost Darlings   28

   Nevers   29

   Scotia's Hero   30

   Mitchell in Mesopotamia   31

   Hassan Bids Farewell to his Love   32

   Politics   33

The Olympians 36
St Andrew's Day 37
Easter Poem 38
La Mer 39
Thieves of Baghdad 40
Do Photos Dream of Paper Birds? 41
Purple I 42
Purple II 43
Dear 5A Classmates, 44
Battle Site 46
Queen of Scots 47
Fashion Notes 48
The Bonnie Hind 49
Reforestation 50
October 51
Home Land 52
Night on the Prairie 53
Camelot Vignette 54
These Times 55
Chinese New Year in Kelvingrove 56
Miracle 57
Love Sonnet XI 58
Love Sonnet XVI 59
Love Sonnet XVIII 60
Love Sonnet LXV 61
Love Sonnet LXXII 62
Spectral Desires 63
An Altitude 64
Tensions 66
Miscalculation 67
Fero City 68
Feli City 69
Tripli City 70
Home Defence, 1943 71
Picnic 72

Mother 74

Passing Places 75

Immemoriam 76

Where Have You Sprung From? 77

Pictures in an Exhibition 78

The Picture of Doreen Gray 79

The Nth Dr Who 80

Hotel C'est La Vie 81

New Purchase 82

Back Gardening by Numbers 83

The Rake 84

From a Distance 85

The Right One 86

Rationalisation 87

Statues 88

Polite Request 89

Fabliau 90

The Last Stories of Kilgore Trout 92

Glasgow Beasts 2: The Next Incarnation 94

Brian Splendid 98

Changing Guard 99

Alphabeat 100

Haibun – To The Deep North 101

Cunning Plan for Honourable Victory 102

Eclogue – In The Gallery 104

Intelligent Design 105

Endangered Species 106

Small Stage 107

Planetary Response 108

By the Way 110

The Falling Apartness of Things 111

the saga of fnc gull 113

the opinions and emissions of fnc gull, larus argentatus

I *In which our hero introduces himself in all his raucous egotism* 114

II *In which fnc gull deplores slanderous imputations* 116

IV   *In which fnc gull discourses on sausages and football*   120
V   *In which our hero bids farewell (with a hint of later return)*   122
the travels and further effusions of fnc gull vagabond extraordinaire 124
I   *In which fnc gull returns with tales of travel*   125
II   *In which our hero meets a formidable mademoiselle*   127
III *In which fnc gull offers a critique of conspicuous consumption* 129
IV   *In which fnc gull begins his homeward flight*   131
V   *In which fnc gull meditates on mortality, religion and beaches* 133
VI   *In which our radical hero stands out against feudal oppression* 135
VII *In which fnc gull makes his will and says his last goodbyes* 137
Redomones   139
The Broch of Glass   140
In Balladia   141
Returning to Lanark   143
Recording for Eddie   145
Morganstern   146
Maighstir Norman   148
Day on the Hill   149
Callanish   150
Sheep in Harris   151
Anger   152
Horatian Ode   153
Remembering Jimmy   154
Big Guy on the Town   156
Lord of the Dance   157
A Hero of the New World   158
Las Cabras *(The Goats)*   *159*
Boatsang   160
Four Sonnets of Garcilaso de la Vega   161
Stone Poem   163
Legend for Sisyphus Stone   164
Turn of the Season   165
Vision   166
Cockcrow   167
Dominus Reconstructus   168

A Good Day for Mr Pepys 170
View from the Gallery Wall 171
Elegy on some Gentlemen of Fortune 173
Hello My Lovely 175
Croque Monsieur 176
Beltane 178
Once Upon a Time in Orcadia 180
The Communication 181
Losing Face 183
American Cross Code 184
Class Outline 185
On the Wireless 186
POTUS Moment 188
The Irruption of Topsy 189
What the Ancients Did for Us —The Picts 190
The Seer of Achnashellach Contemplates Religion 191
Creationists Ahoy! 192
From the Pictish Phrase-book 193
More from the Pictish Phrase-book 194
Grail Quest 195
Sorry, Chaps 197
Monarchs of the Glen 199
Welcome 200
Symposium in the Park with George 201
Social Education Period 202
Royal Wedding 204
BBC Weather Map 205
Perfect Image 206
Muckin Oot the Auld Hame. 208
Cycle Puncture 209
The Sea, The Sea 211
The Who 212
Catcall 213
The Numerous Conjunction 214
Watershed 215

Eye to the Future

I	Better Thegither	218
II	Skipping Chant	219
III	The Right Hon. PM Speaks	220
IV	The Sleep of Reason	221
V	Stop the Press	222
VI	The Question	223
VII	Two Views	224
VIII	Primary Sources	225
IX	Interview with H.M.	226
X	Mirror Image	227
XI	Ingratitude	228
XII	The Human Chain – 11/09/13	229
XIII	Aye, Man, Aye	230
XIV	The Verdict	231

Riding to Trapalanda — **233**

The Passion of Don Roberto — 234
La Pasión de Don Roberto — 235
Trapalanda — 236
Meetin in the Mist — 237
King Robert IV — 238
Esperanzas — 239
R.B. Cunninghame Graham at Glen Aray — 240
Boats on the Lake — 241
Barcos en el Lago — 242
President Graham Speaks to the Nation — 243

Walking to the Island — **245**

Introduction — 246
Prologue: Jeantown — 247
Dail a' Chladaich (The Shore Meadow) — 248
An t-Eilean Sliombagh (The Island) — 256
Island Haiku — 257
Beannachd Leibh (Goodbye, and Blessings on You) — 260

Insular Poems — **265**

Prewar — 266

LMS Inverness-Kyle, 1942.   268
View from the Island   269
Returned Exile   270
A Distant Guitar   271
Grammar Lesson   272
On the Banks of Nith A Dumfries Youth, 1937-60) **273**
42 George Street, Dumfries, 1937-41   274
First Day, 1940   275
Moffat Road, 1941-43   276
Class Photo, 1943   277
Moffat Road, 1943   278
Moffat Road, 1943-46   279
Nissen Hut   280
Staff Sonnets   281
The Arrival of the World.   284
Strangers within our Gates   286
"Rednose", 1947-53   287
Rood Fair, 1952   289
A Daily Walk through History   290
Foresters' Arms, January, mid-1950s   291
On the Buses, Summer 1953, 1954   292
Lochar Moss, Summer 1957   293
Rosemount Street, 1960   295
Sonnets to Hugh MacDiarmid   **298**
Other Scots Poems   **307**
Aff tae Istanbul   308
Lady Gray   309
Lykewake Express   310
Donald, Here's to You, Sir   312
Saga City   313
LOBEY DOSSER RYDZ AGEN   314
The Scottish Patient   315
The Ballad of Archie McGaw   316
A Guid Scots Education   318
A Wearie Fit   320

Laughing at Confucius   **323**

On the Royal Road   324

Sonnet: On Westminster Bridge, 2017   325

Sonnet on the Departed   326

Touché, Touché!   327

Only a game   328

Echoes in the caves of Albion   329

Back in the Tang Dynasty   330

Charlie's Pep Talk   331

Don Roberto's Europe.   333

Haibun   335

Hemispheric   336

Poppies No More   337

Stendhal on a Spanish Balcony   339

Notes — An Altitude Within   *341*

Notes — fnc gull   *343*

Notes — Redomones   *345*

Notes — Eye to the Future   *347*

Notes — Riding to Trapalanda   *348*

Notes — Walking to the Island   *349*

Notes — Insular Poems   *350*

Index   *351*

Biographical Note   *355*

An Altitude Within

The poems in this collection are drawn from the pamphlets, *Kindly Clouds* (2005) and *The Bountiful Loch* (2007), and from later unpublished work. A number of poems have appeared in *The Herald* and *ParaGraphs*, and the poem, "Scotia's Hero", was the winner of the McCash Scots Poetry Prize in 2005.

Black and White

This is how that past remains awake.
After the memories shrug on their macs
And go out into the dark rain,
And all the voices stumble up the stairs
Towards their pillow whispering,

There, on the table with the glasses
And the nibbled snacks in wine-rings,
The images are still spread out,
Pictures of a time before our childhood
And our parents' prime:

The plus-foured golfer in his follow-through,
A smile just forming on his fleshy face;
The first snapshot of the evening out,
He in black tie and playing dutiful squire
To model wife with silver hair and gown
Derived from the latest movie mag;
The girls in summer frocks, the boys in shorts,
Frozen in happiness under the elm;
Black blurred figures on what was once beach
Caught *in extremis* running or falling.

The black, the white, the shades of grey
Still hold the colours of a distant day.

A Seasonal Catalogue

First it is a suspicion.
"That's a black-looking sky, I shouldn't be surprised if — "

Then there is the first sighting.
Sudden speck on the windscreen.
"Is that dandruff on your shoulder?"
Aimless white fly in the air.

Soon it is definite.
"Look, it's snowing." The first of the season
Always surprises, delights some still.
The quiet crumbs from heaven
Sharp against the dark walls.
New coins spilt on the pavement.
A shaking of salt on your hair.

The senses take note.
The even brightness on the bedroom ceiling.
The baffled whush of passing cars.
The snowball scrunching in the fingers.
The instant tingle on the gums.
An almost imagined winter fragrance.

It can keep coming —
Always directly at you in the dipped beam,
Steady sifting as the afternoon wears dim,
Flumps of serious business in the chilly dawn,
Tidy shading out of pages in the colour book.

It presses all the buttons.
I'm dreaming of and jingle bells,
The stagecoach and the robin,
God rest ye merry, Tiny Tim,
Dickens Past and Dickens Yet To Come.

Easy to forget
The sudden moving slope,
The rumble on the loaded scree,
The engulfed corries,
The climber frozen beneath the printless mound,
The stifled sheep behind the drystane dyke.

But soon
We have slush

for ever

whatever
comes to rest upon the foreshore
drifting to the cornices
of noble rooms
sniffed by the wiry urban fox
raising a smile upon a lined and weary face

whoever
sits in certain cafes off the plaza
turning the pages of your latest novel
losing the thread of every argument
walked upon by feral cats
under the temple in the mountain kingdom

whenever
the bell tolls not for thee
and summer thunder crackles after the china cups
the verey rocket lights up no man's land
while fiddlers play
the merry boys of greenland

wherever
into a small cave creeps the anguished mother
the laughing builder checks the level on the rising wall
the empty brandy glass is pushed away
and the last crossword clue is pencilled in
the starlings rise as one into departing flight

however
we receive the reading of our uncle's will
regard the twilight on the wide lagoon
applaud the flautist in madame's salon
or merely contemplate another fall of blossom
reflected in the spotted full-length mirror

whyever
did we smile at yet another insult
stoop to retrieve the silver sixpence on the pavement
engage in talk the stranger in the window seat
decide on americano rather than the latte

never
to sketch the model on the plush chaise-longue
to shoot the sun upon the frigate's heaving deck
to buy the last three strawberry tarts
or hear the final broadcast from the capital
and lift the portrait from the board-room wall   for ever

Night-Town

I walked your streets again last night,
                town of my dreams,
your pavements crowded as they always are,
                it seems.

I recognised the long main street,
                leading somewhere
I had to get to very soon.
                I never reached there.

There were the usual checks along the way:
                the stairs;
a shallow lake to wade; the traffic's rush;
                the dancing bears.

It was, I remember, growing dark,
                the lighted stores
distracting as I hurried past
                their gilded doors.

The fairground lights again blazed up ahead,
                the sea on the right.
Somewhere there are hills. I must avoid
                their fearful height.

I met new people this time on my way,
                the bearded bore,
the foreign-spoken man kicking his helmet,
                an amiable whore.

And, as ever, she whom I should know
                comes to say
those hopeful words I cannot remember
                in the wakeful day.

Forebodings

There have been premonitions.
My neighbour's flowering pear,
so long a summer bonus in
its splendour, was cut down
last year, to be replaced by flag-
stoned drive and plants in pots.
A sleek Bengali cat, superb
in spots and wild electric stare,
refused my proffered stroke
the other day. A traffic cone
adorned (and scratched) the bonnet
of my Astra on a morning
last September.

These things, and others, have
their meaning. Something does portend
I do not wish to meet.
Am I a target then, a new
rogue state for some extra-galactic
superpower? Is a regime change
to my fragile equilibrium
being contemplated in a distant capitol
I have offended?

Whatever,
calmness is indicated,
panic should be avoided,
resistance will probably be useless.

Tomorrow I shall go out as usual,
blinking an amiable optimism,
looking to walk familiar streets
under the kindly clouds,
with only random trepidations
of my semi-daunted heart.

Character

Who are you there in my mind
With your features blank, waiting to be developed
Under the red light, smile or sneer appearing
As the liquid sloshes in the tray,
Like the moment in the film when the killer's face
Takes shape before the girl assistant's eyes?

Are you friend or family,
Or something closer, with your personal data,
All your private parts, assembled
From the fragments in the cellar, crying "Victor!"
As you catch the lightning flash from heaven
Through Igor's apparatus in the scary tower?

What kind of child are you,
Without a childhood or a kindly nurse,
No birth certificate to prove your origin,
No passport to be waved at bored officials?
Are you the Word, or that beneath the Word,
A string of lights within the skull's grey web?

Do you exist for ever now?
I see you take your promenade
Among that other population of your kind,
The folk of dreams, the faces in the curling snaps,
Jane's children, William's greenroom set,
Sir Walter's lost and broken clans.

The Selkie and the Drunks

(after Pablo Neruda, *Fabula de la sirena y los borrachos*).

It was weird, I can tell you,
all of us there in the Whaler's Bar,
when in she comes, totally starkers.
We were all half-pissed, began to whoop and yell.
Just out of the loch, she hadn't a clue,
a selkie who had followed the wrong tideway.
The jeers slipped off her shining skin,
beer and spittle dripped from her opal breasts.
She did not know tears and did not weep;
she knew nothing of clothes and could not dress.
Some stubbed out fags on her, drew on her
with felt-tips, doubled up laughing
and choking.
She said nothing, for she had no language.
Her eyes held the hue of distant love;
her arms seemed shaped as twins of topaz;
her lips were cut from lighted coral.
And suddenly she was gone through the same door.....

The water of the burn cleansed her
in a flash as she slipped in, to gleam
like rainwashed quartz,
and off she swam again, never a look behind,
off towards neverland, off to a dying.

A New Kind of Hero

His greatest crime in their eyes was to win
(refusing that well-known romantic part,
the Nearly Man, the subject of bad art,
a hundred folk songs and a myth wherein

auld Scotland takes it bravely on the chin,
done down by foreign spite and lack of heart
in those at home), to set himself apart
from all the faded Kindred of the Reject Bin

and come out smiling. They could not forgive
the ease with which he set at naught their credo
that Scots are aye fit subjects for regret,

never quite mastering the way to live,
avoided Fate's unseen torpedo
and moved with grace in History's minuet.

From the Gaelic [1]

If I were with you tonight
Sitting on the rocks by the Sound,
I would speak my love into your ear
In the language of our people,
And you would be in no doubt
About the truth and the honesty
And the perfection of my feeling.

Yet since you are there in the Glen of Sanctuary
And I am here in the Davis Strait
Chasing the great whale in the cold seas of Greenland,
I cannot speak my love as I desire.

And so I shall whisper my love's truth
In the face of the western gale,
And publish my honesty
To the white-bonneted waves beneath our keel,
And sing my perfect song
To the young salmon of the sea.

Thus I shall know that on a certain evening,
As you stand by our rock,
The west wind will rustle my love's truth
To your ear in the gentle dark;
And on a morning as you gather
The cockles from the ebb,
The small tide will ripple my clear honesty
Over your bare feet;
And on another day at noon,
Not the least of days,
As you sit by the Fall of the Silver Hair,
The great incoming salmon in its leap
Will trace the perfect line of love's artistry
Against the white water and the grey rock.

In this last way you will be assured
I too will come, if God wills it,
Back to my own river of home,
Bearing my bag of golden dowry in my pack
And our red love safe under my black jacket.

Carranaich[2]

When I was ten or so,
my brother spent hours teaching me
how to say it properly —
'Scare Crackoch' — 'No' —
'Skeer Chrachock'— 'No, you eejit' —
At last it was right.
'Sgeir Chreagach'[3]—another space
filled on the inherited ancestral map.

Many years later, I say to a woman
on the shore of the Ob[4], 'Do you see thon boat?'
'Wot boat?' 'The one out there,
to the right of the Sgeir Chreagach.'
'The wot?' 'The craggy rock out there,
along from the Sgeir Fhada.' [4]
'That rock! It doesn't have a name.'

All the places and the histories dissolve
before the holiday home, retirement cottage,
relocation, relocation on the Costa Minch,
'tabula rasa', slate wiped clean
of all those jawbreaking funny names
that gave a people a belonging sense.
Too much trouble now, when 'Lilac Cottage',
'Mon Repos' and 'Duncommutin'
will fit the bill much better;
while Justin and Tracy, three generations on
from Donnchadh[6] and Seonaid[7],
live all unwary of their loss.

Crowlin Mor [8]

The dinghy slaps the jewelled sea,
The dark island swells ahead.
In silver cups we toast the rising day.
On the vulnerable coast astern
Frail townships expect the worst.

On this island my great-grandfather was the 'King'.
The stones of his house are overgrown with bracken and brambles.
Through the door-space I look over to the mainland glen
From which a mercenary laird drove him
One and a half centuries ago.

Under a kinder sun there would be a lizard on the lichened rock.
But there is no lizard.

The words of Cousin Bill,
They sure must have been pissed-off
To find where they ended up,
A New World view
Of Old World economics.

Between Crowlin Mor and Crowlin Meadhonach
A white bird at anchor.
We pass and wave.
Four incurious alien eyes stare back.

Torridons

Forget winter, all year round
You know how to unnerve:

Sitting in the sun like kindly terrifying grannies,
Brown skirts modest over spread legs
Streaked with droppings and silver slavers;

Distant immaculate in evening dress,
Under chiselled damn-you profiles;

On a bad hair day, tipping the white oblivion
Off the shoulder into your personal space;

Most troubling, in the full grey-out,
As the Tao might say,
Where you see no mountains, there are mountains,

And to prove the point, you touch the nothing
With a darker shadow.

Cathair [9]

My grandfather's black chair
defined his kitchen space
with a kindly order.
He sat in it
(that first memory)
laughing down at me.
Later elsewhere it was a telephone seat
with Laura Ashley cushion.
In another kitchen
its beige cracked paint
is under magazines and dog-hairs.
Soon it will fill
the chair-shaped vacancy
where I write this now.

Uniforms

(Ian MacGillivray, 1900-1943)

The poppies in the lucent jug
Shed their petals fast.
The curtains stir in the autumn breeze,
The sunshine cannot last.

My spectacles lie on the table,
The pure china glows.
The photos tell their story
To the son who knows.

A young Gordon Highlander,
Trained fit and keen,
Saved by the peace of November
In Nineteen-Eighteen.

A middle-aged Home Guard private,
With office and family:
It was Senior Service and Craven 'A'
Got him in Forty-Three.

So who do you think you're kidding, Mr Hitler,
If you think we're having fun?
Captain Mainwaring, Private Fraser,
Each with his pack and gun,
You don't need enemy bullets
To be undone.

Sonnet

Through East and South and North and West I see
Our love has flourished in the changing breeze,
Knowing its own precise geography
Mapped out in streets and hills and seas.

Auld Reekie saw companionable walks
After the studies of the day were done;
The Borders held more close and loving talks
And love was sealed beneath the London sun.

The Highland mountains and the Shetland sea
Witnessed the rapture of parental joys;
The West has woven us a tapestry
Of pride and loss and grief in equipoise.

Upon this shifting ground my trustful heart
Relies on you as its unfailing chart.

The Owl and the Pussycat

They were an ill-assorted couple, people thought,
by any standards: he with his wide-eyed gaze
and silent walk; she with that cuddly pose
and egocentric purr.
How they clicked is anyone's improbable guess;
the whole world knows the rest.

Where did the fur and feathers meet? Perhaps
on night-time prowl, each with an eye for prey,
under the moony lights of Hunter's Disco
or at the roulette wheel of Forest Glade Casino?
Did they swoop and pounce upon the same
small victim, but find a greater fascination in each other,
and let their mousy target flee to safe conventional arms?

That cruise they booked, wasn't that something else?
The Emerald Princess, made for romance, dressed
over all, aglide upon an eastern sea,
heading for Coromandel and the Coast of Spice,
with starlight serenades, lavish dispensing of his
laundered wealth, the stateroom raptures (making much use
of honey, our steward source reports), all leading
to her untypical demand to make it legal.

And so the ring, of local gold, bought in the bazaar
(at favourable discount, he being as he is), the ceremony
conducted by an imam, no less (how too exotic, darlings!),
and the wedding feast purveyed by Coromandel's
most prestigious curry palace. And far, far
into the scented night, while sitars played and drums
provided throbbing echoes to their hearts,
under the constellations of the south
and the inevitable comes-with-the-package moon,
along the glowing, net-hung beach,

he, with his solemn cruelty-concealing stare
and stiff-legged prance, and she, all yawning,
stretching, sinuous complacency, paced out
their saraband, caught in amoral taloned ecstasy.

Reid [10]

O, reid the leaves upo the girss
　An reid the rowan berry,
But reider yit the scarf you wore
　Upo the island ferry.

We walked alang the open deck
　An mindit days of gold.
The sun went doun into the wast,
　The sea grew dark and cold.

Whaur did the lauchter gae yon day,
　The easy smiles thegither?
Somewhere atween the licht and dark
　I saw them fade and wither.

The years are lang, the years are grey,
　The sea is aye atween,
An you are on the ither shore
　Whaur I hae rarely been.

But come the morrow's morn I'll rise
　An tak the island ferry,
An lay reid roses on your grave
　Aneath the rowan berry.

Lunar Eclipse

No longer do we think about you much;
you've always been around, above the scene,
looking aloof, disdainful of the touch

of mundane business that might demean
that pure intensity, the slightly fake
illusion of a being divine, serene.

We've never been convinced, could not quite take
your box of tricks: the full-face wide-eyed stare;
the crescent wink; the pudgy ageing rake;

the dodgy juggling of clouds and air
to tease the viewer with your half-concealed,
half-flaunted charms. Quite frankly, we don't care.

Perhaps, at times, the shimmering path revealed
across the sea; another night, the stark
unsculpted marble on the wide bed's field;

the enigmatic shadows in the park:
these sound a chord, pierce deep enough
to stop the breath. But then whatever spark

you strike is stifled by that goddess stuff,
thou queen and huntress, mistress of the night,
the claptrap of the classics, antique bluff

of holy nonsense spreading moss and blight
across reality. We like to think the truth;
the face you show us as a virgin light

is hot as hell, and marred with dust and drouth,
the rear you hide more frigid than the pole,
and as for mystery or romance, forsooth,

you've less of that than any lump of coal
or candlewax. And yet, no doubt, you'll keep
the act upon the road, the aureole

well polished, rob the audience of their sleep
each night, cavorting on your silver crutch,

from **Two Native Lands — A Love Song** [12]

("Dos paises—canción de amor")

> *Viejo río de barcos*
> *y de revolución fracasada.......*

Old river of ships
and failed revolution,
Clyde, in my second land
of Scotland,
let me explain some things
to you about my first land,
Spain, mother of sorrows
and bleeding memories.
On your bank
beside a busy bridge,
La Pasionaria
extends her arms,
saluting Glasgow's worker-soldiers
of an old brigade.
My father heard her speak
in words of fire
before the Fascist winter
fell.......

See my guitar
here on my knee,
both old and warped.
Manuel Delgado said,
"Hold this for me, chico,"
and then two Civil Guards
led him round the corner;
I heard the shots
as I ran home.
When I play this now,
in Granny Black's
or in the Scotia Bar,
I think of two old men
with spotted hands,
drinking their Soberanos
in our new democracy,
talking of Franco,
and Manuel and I
combine our spirits
to create the Spanish mood
your Scottish languages

Departing

When you call me, as you will,
into the sunlit study, and,
standing between the filing-cabinets,
say that, yes, for me the day has come,

all that remains to do will be to choose
provisions for the journey, a book
or two, perhaps a fine old malt,
and who, out of the many, will companion me.

I can hear the arguments then, the woman
in the beret insisting she be excused,
he with the cold smile chiding her,
but both deferring to the shy collector

of Victoriana as a schooldays chum.
Yet, at the last, I'll board that high-decked ship
with one who signals a desire to come,
not for any thought of me, but merely

on a whim of novelty, the big adventure,
shouldering her bag, tossing her scarf
undaunted to the freshening breeze
and the emerging sea.

i

Flower Power

Look at the flowers, how they con you
with their garish faces, delicate bodies
and the innocent perfume; all their allies
too in herbals and aromatherapy
courses. See when you have them cut
and rearranged *à japonaise* around the long-
stemmed vase to stand upon the polished
rosewood escritoire, how they deceive
as to their global destiny.

Back in the borders and the island beds, out
in the nurseries, round the walled garden
with its haunted moon-gate, the conclave
of the tangled roots and eloquent capillaries
continues heedless of the passing worms.
Aloft the nuzzling bee, glutted with nectar,
pollen-brushed, flies off unwary of the coded
messages he bears to foreign parts.

Perhaps the date has been already set, Der Tag,
the F-Day, when you wake to find it done and dusted,
the Botanic Revolution, with the storming of the greenhouse
and the garden-shed. How will it feel
to be arraigned and sentenced by the rainbow court,
led to an execution signalled
      by the trumpets of the daffodil,
            and duly carried out
                  by tulips' graceful spears,
                        the pansies' Gorgon stares,
                              the wicked daggers of the rose?

Signs of the Day

You do not feel the day's stigmata come
so much as think them to erupt
suddenly upon the morning light
when birdcalls signal yet another waking
and foxes head for home
along suburban streets. You study
in the bedroom mirror how the opening
slash under the right nipple drips
quick blood upon the toilette brushes
and the thumbprints on the ribcage
darken to reveal the whorls and loops
which match (you know) the hands
of her you casually betrayed
those years ago. They will be gone
by night, you comfortlessly tell
yourself, applying the plasters
and the soothing gel. Put on concealing
tee-shirts, sweaters, soft flamboyant fleeces.
Face the day, and brave the indifferent
morning observation of the world.
Yes, sure enough, at the calm centre
of the afternoon, you leave your desk
and in the empty washroom
hitch up the top towards your cold
and drying throat. See how
your chest, unmarked beneath a fading tan,
rises and falls with slowing breaths
almost in disappointment at the passing
of the miracle, the signs.

Adjust your dress, move on.
Attend with patience
        the infallibly wounding night.

Coming Ashore

What country, friends, is this?
                    Illyria, lady.
And what should I do in Illyria? [13]

The coming-ashore reception sets the mood:
not the gliding cruise-ship progress
    through an archipelago of summer havens,
nor the fearful pre-dawn edging
    towards an unlit problematic coast;
not the eager scanning with world-wearied eyes
    for childhood landmarks,
nor the gasping final flounder through the surf
    and clutching backwash.

Rather the Port Band blowing 'Colonel Bogey',
    displaying CDs and huge-peaked hopeful hats;
the striding piper on the dockside
    to stir returning exiles' hearts;
the opening-up of mortars and machine-guns
    from cruel unsurprised redoubts;
the blissful sprawl on sun-hot sand
    ready for Prince to come
        with fluttering shirt and stately stallion,
    or wide-eyed Princess and her ladies
        gathering shells.

The Interlude [14]

In the Garden

At this hour of mid-afternoon,
on this day of mid-July,
the shadows creep across the lawn
under the dart of the house martin
and the lumbering bee.
Hundreds of miles to the South,
the body parts are still emerging
from under Kings Cross,
delivered from the heat and the rats;
hundreds of miles to the North,
the islands of the world
compete in amity
amid the windy skerries
along the barely-ending day.
It is an interlude in the way
that most things are,
coming after and before,
between hither and hence,
holding the remembered/
                     forgotten
and the unforeseen/
                     expected.
It is special because it is,
and already it has been.

In the Hall of the Inquisitor

wherever and after
they go beyond
do we say the going
has a for
and a therefore

what do we
contemplate
in that aforemath
that makes

should the sea
recharge its meaning
and the hills relapse into their mood
of subtle disengagement

et après tout
is there the
what
and whyfore
to determine
the utterness of deprivation.

Lost Darlings

At the conference buffet,
along from salad sandwiches
and vegetarian samosas,
but before the mini-sausages on sticks
and chicken goujons,

a tray of tiny white things
perched upon square-inch bits of toast –
"cured herring canapés," a label says –
a moment's bite, then melts for ever.
This is not how it was.

A dozen gleaming bars go flop into the pail
out of the salted boxes in the Kintail van.
Here's another two, you're a growing lad.
I hand him Granny's money, genuine
silver shilling with the bearded head.

On the kitchen table,
beside the bowl of floury bursting tatties
and the butter dish,
a blackened pan full of the bent
boiled goodness, drained of brine.

Disdaining cutlery, we pick
white flesh. The skeletons pile up
like Korky the Cat's picnic.
On the meal-kist, still-warm bannocks,
crowdie in its cabbage-leaf,

crab-apple jelly lie in wait.
Past the hen-house,
out beyond the Island
a school of sliding porpoises
go joyous through the bountiful loch.

Nevers

so many nevers crowd in upon
the autumn years to brush
in passing on the escalator

to see the earth from space
to hold her child before the smiling camera
to hit that satisfying six

a white sail skims northwest before Morvern
a wild-eyed pheasant pecks at bright young grass
a hoodie rises from its fence-post

to place a stone upon the last Munro
to make the witty speech as father of the bride
to part the bow from long-held note

the wind's effect is what we see
white tops white sail running free
labouring crow wings branches in distress
elegant gull in still suspension
by the ferry's upper deck

to sign the charter on a polished table
to give a daughter willingly away
to write the poem that will change a life

I find these coloured beads around the floor
the wren's quick movement on the myrtle twig
a trusting snail upon the busy pavement
small voice that moment before waking
saying daddy

Scotia's Hero [15]

Gret *Wallace*, hero ye maun be to those
Quha think oure lichtlie o thir landis fame,
Greitan lyk bairnis to think hou *Scotlandis* foes
Thy giantis bodie cruellie did maim
And caa it tressoune to proude *Edwardis* name
That ye to keip your countree puir and free
Did cause gret strife and bluidie *English* shame.
Yet hero, martir, are ye nane to me.
Had ye but gien *Plantagenet* the knee
And hailed him *Scotlandis* prince and richtfu lord,
Than had there been a *British* reaulme to see
Thrie hunder year afore my kingly sword.
Than wald baith landis ha seen the blyssins poure
Fra ferrest *Orknays* to the *Scilly* shore.

Thairfor I claim your title as my ain,
Me, *Jamy Stewart*, saxt and first by richt,
Hero for this newe age, regnand by my pen,
Spreidin threwch time to come baith leir and licht.
First I bequeathe to alle this nobill sicht,
Britain united, free fram auld disdains;
The neist, my plan for *Scripture* scrievit bricht,
Ane tung for *Scottis* and *Suddrons* baith at anis;
And last, to spite the cateran *Irishe* trains,
A godlie *Scottis* plantation in the *North*.
Thrie recipes to ease aa social paines,
And fetch *Fortunas* happie sperritis forth.
Thus, *Wallace, Time* dissolves your martial rage
And crounes me Makar o the Future Age.

James Stewart
King of England and of Scots,
soi-disant King of Great Britain.
1605.

Mitchell in Mesopotamia [16]

Lying on your barracks cot,
hearing the bugle singing "Sunset"
to the sinking flag above the dusty parks
of fobbed-off Faisal's fake new kingdom,

could you imagine – beyond your embryo
Chris and Ewan, beyond Blawearie's stooks,
after the songs, the War, the firing squad –
the Flowers of yet another Forest

culled with bombs and ambush
down the sun-parched road that leads to Basra,
North Highlanders defending a corrupted cause,
marched to the pipes another standing milestone

further from the Golden Age?

Hassan Bids Farewell to his Love

A Ghazal. [17]

City of Peace, you feed my sight each morning as the sun's new light
Floods in to put the dark to flight, and show your beauty clear, Baghdad.

Haroun the Caliph in disguise goes forth by night to hear the cries
Of fools and laughter of the wise, among his people of Baghdad.

Did he but ask me, I could tell how it is Paradise and Hell
To live beneath a city's spell, the curse of loving you, Baghdad.

Since living here eats up my soul, diverts me from the scholar's scroll,
And plunges me in wine's full bowl, what can I do but go, Baghdad?

Now at the Eastern Gate I stand, ready to tread, with staff in hand,
The Golden Road to Samarkand, the exile's path from my Baghdad.

And if they told me you had died, your towers smashed, your grace denied,
What might I do but cry they lied, and turn away in tears, Baghdad?

Politics

How can they not scent it all around,
hovering like musk, a cloud of sensuous meaning,
this multi-coloured youth with studs, tattoos
and hip-dependent floppy trousers
under junk-food midriffs,

shutting it out with urgent ringtones,
their summons to communion with the genies
of the air, in trains, in parks,
along the social streets?

While shirtsleeved statesmen fill
the unwatched screens,
agonise for turn-out,
stretch their desperate hands for votes
beyond the faithful grey retainers
of democracy.

What would it take to raise the orange flags
in plazas, wave the roses,
fill the stadiums
with solemn youthful choristers
who hold each others' hands,
catching the fragrance of a different world
that tugs and whispers,
"This can be yours
if only......"?

Firth of Clyde

South of Gourock
a gannet soars
folds blacktipped wings
and punches deep
into the grey water

Another predator
pushes its black sail
ready to disappear
punching deeper
into the same grey

Not the Real Thing

Those who emerge from the enduring night
May look with joy at the dim half-light,
Singing out praise of the new day's birth,
Before beginning to question its worth,
Not knowing the hills yet hide from view
The sun's full blaze awaiting its cue.

The Olympians [18]

What are our 'beautiful lofty things?'
Not such aristocrats as Yeats admired,
Actors and drunks and stately women
Standing out against the mediocre troubled times.

Rather MacDiarmid's contemplation of the thistle;
"A man's a man" sung full in Mrs Windsor's face;
A Parliament and damn the cost; Gray's
Lanark at his end; the wide embrace
By Morgan of a cosmos for his pen;
Old Don Roberto on his pampas steed;
Madame Ecosse in Strasbourg; the Cuillin
Under a winter sun; John Smith among the kings
Beneath Iona's turf: our true Olympians,
Such things as we may hope to see again.

St Andrew's Day

The day began much as might be expected;
No bright dawn, some cloud and blows of rain.
By breakfast, sun in patches, bits of blue.

The forenoon brought some clearer weather,
People in better spirits, expecting a fine day,
Although some showers, the place being where it was.

During the lunch-hour, skies turned dreich.
After a heavy plump, the grey cloud settled down,
And we all thought, *That's it then, till the night.*

All went about their business, not put out greatly
By the unencouraging light — it could be borne.
Some grew to like it, who needs the sun?

What a surprise to find the forecasts wrong,
The dullness but an interlude, a lightening sky.
Though some resented it, the change did come.

And now, full afternoon, white clouds, a breeze.
No startling burst of gold, yet time to walk.
Best take a brolly. Still the air is clear.

Is that a patch of sunlight on the hill?
Could be a fine evening, not a bad day after all.

Easter Poem

If Spring were a once-a-century event,
Would we know to recognise it
As the miracle it is —
La dolce primavera, pleasant king
Of all the wintry, sultry decades
Coming before and after?

It should come with wondrous certitude,
However long delayed, matching ecstatic
Memories caught in the fading ink
Of great-grandparents' journals,
Telling of primroses and lambs
And freshest greens imaginable.

And if Easter too belonged to only
One week-end per hundred years,
An afternoon of agony, two days in dark,
An early morning when the sealing stone
Is moved and myth emerges
To contort reality, should we not

Dismiss it as a freak? How could faith
Remain alive across the untransforming
Years, without the steady sensuous parade
Of ritual habits, blurry choral
Nonsense, nostril-gripping incense,
Mesmeric antique words?

Some things need a desperate re-reminding,
Others, more assured, come always
Unannounced and opportune.

La Mer [19]

La Mer — not the Debussy take,
but Trenet's. Ten minutes on the train,
writing on toilet paper, Paris to Narbonne,
a song is born.

La Mer — how you evoke the Northern
Frenchman's summer dream! Route Nationale
in August vers le Midi, lazy shores of the Golfe du Lion,
flocks of angelic clouds.

La Mer — yours are the silver reflections
under the rain, the pools of reeds,
the crumbling houses and the drifting gulls,
lulling the heart with love.

La Mer — your waters lap a vanished shore;
in each faubourg, the rippling pianos,
smooth pomaded singers, spill on to the pavements
from the smoky cafe-bars.

"Je ne peux pas vous oublier...
   (missing the roads to freedom,
     trudging to Compiègne,
      stumbling to Vichy,
       cheering mon Général,
        cloaking a national guilt)
depuis que les bals sont fermés."

In a song of love, the sea consoles my heart.

Thieves of Baghdad [20]

Where are you when we need you, Sabu,
with your magic carpet to carry us to freedom?

The old Sultan is dead in shock and awe
from the many daggers out of the air.

The mountain-high Afreet from the bottle
has been targeted by smart bombs.

The young Caliph has regained his sight
and leads the insurgents against the Green Zone.

The blue rose that will restore the Princess
is crushed beneath the desert boots of grunts.

The great spider in its web behind the temple idol
aches in longing for the blood on the city streets.

The miraculous flying horse is shot by Apaches
from the sky above the minarets.

The bazaars are empty of the breads and fruits,
the nuts and spices of Arabia.

The wicked Vizier Jaffar with his hypnotic eyes
falls, a black stone, into the Tigris.

Was it better, Sabu, when you were enchanted
to a dog's shape and cringed under a cruel foot?

Bear us away, young master, to the clean desert
and the Oasis of Oblivion.

Do Photos Dream of Paper Birds? [21]

This future is uncomfortably close,
fiction already being born as fact.
"Is that owl real?" "Of course not."
Emotional response is what you lacked,

revealing you too as cloned, illegal,
proper target for the cop with gun.
In rain-lashed streets the immigrant crowds
supplant the cars, the rats have run

to pricey offshore havens, fine apartments
left to squatting and decay.
Who are the heroes, who the humans? –
licensed killer who has lost the way,

company secretary who has lost her past,
genetics geniuses lonely in their towers,
android superman who finds a soul
in his final pre-planned hours?

"All those moments lost
like tears in rain."
A dove escapes the easing fingers.
Time to die – again.

Purple I

Then I branded the Caesars with my costly shellfish dye,
setting the style for all imperial shows of might;
whether the thumb was up or down,
my tincture sealed its right.

Now I provide the oohs and ahs for TV shows,
where giggling Linda, lofty Laurence each supplies
the master bedroom with its colour scheme,
opening the tins to fake surprise.

What I could have been was foiled by Chance.
Ah, had you but seen
the high-strung Captain Mauve destroy the Mysterons,
that Tarantino hero, bloodsoaked Mr Aubergine.

Purple II

If I should trespass on your patch,
Will you forgive my prose upon the page,
Allow a flutter with the emperor,
Protect me from the riders of the sage?

And will your rose of Cairo's thorns
Keep the people-eater's jaws apart?
  Forgive my not being born in you,
  And for my bravery give me your heart.

Dear 5A Classmates, [22]

this is Noor, remember, writing to you
from sunny Pakistan. Hope you're all
enjoying life in grey old Glasgow.

Bet you wish you were here, far
from boring maths and chemistry,
slogging away to get to Uni and be medics.

I'm having a great time, helping Mum-in-law
around the house, out with the other women
in Rashid's father's fields, making baby clothes.

That's the big news, I'm going to be a mum.
Rashid and his Dad are very pleased with me,
family duty duly done, mega deal.

That's why they've let me write to you,
sharing the joy. Just the best present
for my birthday – sweet fertile seventeen.

My own Mum and Dad are over the moon.
Makes it all worthwhile. It wasn't half a surprise
last summer holiday here when Dad said

I was to stay and marry Rashid. Yes, I did cry
a bit, but it was fixed already,
big family event, all in Urdu, dead scary.

Rashid's OK, though, pretty dim, Special Needs
case, I would say. But he does his best
and I've got used to it.

Maybe I'll get home some time
and see you all. Dad's got plenty room,
what with his new extension, paid for by Rashid's Dad,

I think. Space for me and baby Ghulam.
It has to be a boy, of course. Then we'll have fun.
Really miss the old scene, the gang,

the clubs, the cafés, all the music buzz.
Write to me, somebody, send me some books
and magazines. Could use an i-Pod.

Funny how life turns out. There was I
dreaming of Dr Noor, white coat, saving
the world. And yet all this was really mine –

the family path, tradition, a life apart
in guarded virtue, knowing my place
and who knows best.

Battle Site [23]

I

Aye, it wis a gey dreich day on yon God-blastit muir,
Eftir the lang merch frae Nairn, drawn up in files,
Us in the third, I'm gled tae say, way back ahint
The real bluidy business when it burst upon us.
Whit can I tell yi, no much fur us tae see,
Aa the Hielan savages skriechin their slogans,
Munro's an Barrel's men butcherin the deils
Wi their tricky bayonet wark. Didnae tak lang.
Then the usual English officer says, aa posh an cool,
"Send some Jocks out to finish them off. Give our lads
A breather." Sae me an Billy Jardine frae Maxwelltoun,
An a couple mair, trots oot owre the heather. Faith,
It wis warth the hingin aboot. Got really stuck intae it.
Slide the bayonets in, watch their een blink oot, "Tak yon,
Yi Papish tink." Plenty bluid tae wipe aff. A real guid day.

II

It wis sae hot the day we went tae Culloden
Yi could see the tar meltin oan the road.
The kids were fair gaspin in the back ae the caur,
We wir gled tae get tae the Visitors' Centre
An hae a drink an an ice-cream. We daunert oot
Tae see the battlefield, bit ae history like.
Aa the stanes fur the deid, Clan Chattan, Clan
McThingummy, an the wee markers fur where
The armies stuid. Maks it really come alive.
Sis wis a bit tearfu, still thinkin aboot Alec
Deid in Afghanistan. No easy fur her.
Me, I tellt the kids, this is your country's past.
See, yi kin feel prood, like, being Scottish.

Queen of Scots [24]

Immured for decades
by her dull-faced
duty-loving
English counterpart,
she, at the end, it's said,
welcomed the freeing stroke
that tumbled long red hair
from underneath
the tight white coiffure,
detached her lengthened shadow
from the dumpy frame,
and sent the yapping corgis
packing from the weighted skirts.

Fashion Notes

You wear the garden most becomingly
today, my love. There have been days
when it was Auntie Rose's too-discordant
over-fussy ball-gown caught in to fit you
with some half-concealed and dubious devices,
encouraging you to prink and flounce,
swishing it around in polka measures.

Once or twice, in winter, it has been serviceable
drab, like overalls or cleaning-out-the-jumble gear,
diminishing you to gardener's apprentice.

Last autumn, for a week or two, it had a trim
unostentatious go-to-meeting slightly soulless
gravity that shut you in to mere convention.

Today, however, as I said, all fits,
becomes, enhances.
The blossoming cherry is the backlight
to your hair. You settle the hedge
around your shoulders with a practised shrug.
The lawn discovers its vocation as a train.
And when you turn to me with humorous lips,
in beds and borders, planters and pots,
the multi-coloured tops and skirts,
scarves and accessories, strut the catwalk
in cascading flowers. Yves St-Laurent
is ousted, Balmain bested,
Dior in eclipse.

The Bonnie Hind [25]

The prince sat in his palace ha'
Wi' sorrow early and late.
The auld queen mither said tae her son,
Tis ye maun find a mate.

A siller hind cam doun the ben,
Wi' grace and beauty fine.
The prince has wedded her in haste
And taen her in her prime.

And a' the land rejoiced tae see
The siller hind sae bien,
For she has stawn oor prince's hert
And she sall be oor queen.

Yet cam the day, a derksome day,
And o but it was drear,
The hind's blue een looked sad and wae
And drapped a bitter tear.

"O, I hae dreamed an unco dream,
Ayont the southern sea.
I saw the hounds cam at my back
And pu'ed me doun tae dee."

Ae nicht the elfin hunt rade oot,
They rade by nicht and day,
And a' the hounds o the western wind
Ran tae catch their prey.

They hae chased her roun the bens,
And owre the southern sea.
Till they hae gruppt her in a cave
And pu'ed her doun tae dee.

O waes me for the siller hind,
And her beauty cruellie torn.
The bluid rins doun her silken sides
For a' the warld tae mourn.

Her prince has taen anither mate,
And smiles on ane and a'.
The hind lies neath a marble stane
Safe fra the hoodie craw.

Reforestation

Watching the sudden forest loom at hand,
As, self-deludingly, we never thought it could,
Our evening walks acquire an edgy mood,
Hearing the exiled beasts reclaim that land

We felt was ours, beaver toppling trees,
Wolf answering wolf, a snuffling choleric boar
Crossing our path, faint heart-stopping roar
Of fabled aurochs carried on the breeze.

Sightings are rare and disconcerting, though:
 The mottled shadow of what could be lynx;
A wheeling vulture; worst, blank-faced as sphinx,
A bear's brown bulk advancing tall and slow.

We made this outlaw world, where we must crouch,
Fearing these licensed monsters' swaggering slouch.

October

You really miss out big time
in the sexy calendar stakes.
No one admires you smiling
saucily out of the fake furs
beside the mulled wine
and mincepies
under the mistletoe.
You don't come skipping
in flimsy draperies over the fields
scattering blossoms and daffs
and showing the odd tattoo.
You don't stretch out languorously
in the rose-garden radiating
a long day's heat and held-in lust.
Even your close sister November
sizzles with flames and fireworks.
There may be a whiff of witchcraft
about you as the dark comes down,
but we can guess you've already
looked out the sensible boots
and there's a warm woollie
ready to put on when the wind
gets up at the clear day's end
and shoos the last rattling
leaves along the frosting street.

Home Land

Soon forgotten –

the guarded welcome
stand in line
obey the unsmiling women
offer up
your finger
your eyeball
your passport
your most secret reasons —

when you rise from the tunnel
into the familiar twilit isle
a hundred towers
a million lights
every street a song
Woody's Manhattan
blue Gershwin sax
wailing you
home

Night on the Prairie

Speeding headfirst over Iowa,
Amtrak stainless steel
Six inches from my nose.

Hands folded on the breast,
(Prayers for the dear departed)
as the upper bunks on the upper deck

sway and throb in sympathy
with the miles-long freight train's
vibes how many miles beyond

the planed horizon. A melancholy
hooting from the lovesick engines
greets each level crossing.

Denver in the morning.

Camelot Vignette

Don't flannel me about History.
Believe me, I was there
when J. Edgar Hoover danced
a rumba with George Chakiris,
and Fidel Castro held their hats.
That was a thing to see, boyo.
JFK said he had a sore back
and opted out of the ladies' excuse-me,
but Jane Fonda begged him
to give her a twirl.
Marilyn was sick as a parrot
when they disappeared
into the Phoenix Park,
swore to Chicago Sam [19]
she'd never trust an Irishman again.
Capisce, he said.

Top of the morning to you,
Father O'Flynn,
there's Old Glory for you.

These Times

So what of these circling days,
the clouds on hold, the blue sky
stuck on standby? Watch this space,
I say, you never know what's
looming on the weather map.
Down the casual street
where whistling crisp-shirted
up-and-comers segway
slickly past the shuffling
bag-people, see, there are many
changes in the offing.
For example,
what is this approaching
through the blue jacaranda haze?
Can it be joy?

Chinese New Year in Kelvingrove

Sunday lunchtime and the families are in.
The Money God hands out red packets, blue
Scottish eyes smiling under a golden crown.
The two-man lion prances through the Colourists,
past Sir Roger's [27] trunk under the Spitfire, leading
a train of silk-pyjamaed dancers round and back
to where the kids cut paper lanterns and the parents
click their mah-jong tiles on cafeteria tables.
Old ladies chat in Cantonese over muffins
and lattes. Four nervous divas mime
to Peking Opera CDs. Gong and cymbals
and applause break out sporadically.
Here in Glasgow stirs the faintest farthest puff
of an awakening dragon's mighty breath.

Miracle

(Healing of a Lunatic Boy, painting by Stephen Conroy, 1986)

What is this healing?

I did not come through
the circus tent of madness
with the beasts in suits of light
to endure this jug-eared bawler
of 'Nessun Dorma' with his hand
on a lapel, his pebble-glassed
attendant, and the indifferent
standers-by.

Where is the carpenter
with desert eyes,
the dawn wind on his hand,
that I was promised?

Enough. I shall rise now
in my troubling
         naked
            sanity.

Love Sonnet XI [28]

(Pablo Neruda, *Tengo hambre de tu boca, de tu voz, de tu pelo...*)

I am famisht fur yir mou, yir voce, yir hair.
I gang quaiet wioot remeid alang the streets.
Breid staps nae the pangs, the daydaw braks me,
by day I seek the ripplin soun o yir feet.

I lang fur yir glidin lauch,
yir hauns wi the hues o hervest lowe.
I'm hungert fur yir pale stanes o fingernails.
I want to crinch yir skin laek a haill hazelnut.

I want tae eat yir beauty's birnan sunlicht,
yir prood hard face's royal neb.
I want tae eat the fleein shadow o yir breers.

An I come an gang, hungrily sniffin the gloamin,
huntin, huntin you an yir het hert
laek a wullcat on the toom Muir o Rannoch.

Love Sonnet XVI

Pablo Neruda, *Amo el trozo de tierra que tu eres....*

I lue the nievefu o erd ye are,
wi yir warldwide prairies
I hae nae ither ster. Ye mak real
the expandin universe tae me.

Yir wide een haud the ainly licht
I ken frae the slockened clans o sters,
yir huil dirls laek the rod
the fire-flaucht merks i the blatter.

Yir hurdies were sae muckle o the mune,
yir deep mou wi its delichts sae muckle o the sun,
sae muckle birnan licht, like hinnie i the byke,

yir bleezin hert in lang reid straiks.
An sae I rin ma kisses owre yir bodie's fire,
ma planetoid, ma mappamound, ma doo.

Love Sonnet XVIII

(Pablo Neruda, *Por las montañas vas como viene la brisa...*)

Ye gang ower the bens laek a snell breeze
or the burn gushin fra neath the snaw,
yir flichterin linn o hair reflects
the heich cloods that adorn the sun.

Aa the licht o the Cuillin faas upo yir bodie
as on a wee jaur that niver fills,
whaur the watter cheynges ay its gear and sang
wi ilka movement o its glessy rin.

Aneath the auld clansmen's path thro the corries
the rushin watter glints laek a claymore
grupped atween waas o a rocky cleuch:

till sudden ye receive fra the wuids
a spray, a flaucht, o bluebells
lowsin the antrin arra o their muirlan scent.

Love Sonnet LXV

(Pablo Neruda, *No estes lejos de mi un solo día, porque como...*)

Dinnae gang awa sae faur, no even fur a single day, because,
ach, I dinnae ken hoo tae say it – a day is lang
an I'll be waitin fur yi, like in a lanely station
whan the trains are sleepin soun awa some ither bit.

Dinnae lea me, no even fur a single oor, because
in yon oor the wee watchful draps'll aa rin thegither,
an perhaps the reek that gangs luikin fur a hame
'll come tae smoor ma wandert hert.

I pray yir shape may neer brak in pieces on the sand,
yir eelids neer flee aff intae the void.
Dinnae gang awa, no fur a second, ma ainly luve,

cause in yon meenit yill hae gane sae faur
I'll cruise ower aa the erd, spierin
gin yill come back or lea me alane tae dee.

Love Sonnet LXXII

(Pablo Neruda, *Amor mío, el invierno regresa a sus cuarteles...*)

My luve, winter merches back tae barracks,
earth sets doon its yalla gifts,
an rinnan oor hauns ower faur-aff lands,
we feel the globe's saft pelt.

Gang aff! Awa this verra day! Wheels an boats an bells,
planes made scherp by endless licht o day
intil lang-grained ears o hervest
towards the islands' waddin fragrance.

C'moan, up ye get an fix yir hair,
take-aff an landin, rin wi the air an sing wi me,
board the trains tae Arabia or Kyle,

nocht but a ferry tae the distant pollened shore,
hert-piercin touns o puirtith an gardenias
rewled by raggedy barefit queens.

Spectral Desires

Between red and orange
Flames delineate fireside rug

Between orange and yellow
Sun-hot sand defines remembered beach

Between yellow and green
Spring quickens in a private garden

Between green and blue
Salty decks inhale shifting sea

Between blue and purple
Summer hazes gentle hills

Between purple and red
Heat-seeking bodies flare their intimate night

An Altitude [29]

How could your book, Michelle, not but succeed?
— the fluttering prayer-flags on the high plateau
clear skies above the awesome mountain greed

and lust within the board-room far below
the swaying bridge white river rush a fear
a loss of confidence you dare not show

the poring over maps sour local beer
loud cloud of flies around the privy tent
bright shaft of dawn that drew and froze a tear

did you not say yon winter day we spent
walking the Campsies how the very light
was ice in essence primal virtue lent

by far-off cold stars as a purge of spite
and overheated passion I did not
go all the way with that a faintly trite

comparison I felt and yet the thought
had power upon the page when first I read
the copy sent me to review it caught

that breathless lips half parted tilted head
approach to life you bring to all you do
I saw how mind and will combined and sped

along the world's high roof to shoulder through
the glazing cold and gulp the air beyond
a Shangri-La the message in the blue

invisible notes of bells the newly dawned
awareness of an altitude within
oneself unclimbed potential to respond

to avalanches of the ego win
or lose to see the peaks the crest reveals
to hear the icemelt torrent's distant din

secure inside your red tent as night steals
across the campsite you will make your notes
by torchlight evidence for the appeals

to save the forests yaks or mountain goats
from bureaucrats repeat the words of calm
and dream how from the knowing dark that floats

above the firm remembered lips bring balm
to tired fartravelled limbs and softly feed
the ears with music of an amorous psalm.

Tensions

It seemed they were always
at verbal cross-purposes.
For her the present was simple,
whereas he dealt in the conditional.
Her aims ran in the continuous mode
and his were quite indefinite,
not to say infinitively split.
Her shalls and shoulds ran constantly
against his mays and mights.
Her visions were indicative
of present perfect,
future perfect,
gosh yes, pluperfect even.
He operated in a different mood,
where, were it but the case,
in would creep the weaselly subjunctives
to cast their doubts.

This could not last.
Time, with its clear imperatives,
made all their conjugations
definitely past,
historic.

Miscalculation

He always had a way with figures,
Doing the working in his head,
Making relationships,
Getting the right results.

It was a definite plus, a positive,
He found her in the same line,
And, putting one and one together,
Came up with his answer.

Nothing could subtract from the sum
Of their parts, the total of their primes.
Much was carried over,
Leaving, it seemed, no remainder.

Times and times again
They magnified their feelings,
Passions multiplying to infinity,
An unimagined product.

Time, however, the great divisor,
Goes into everything, a last improper fraction,
Cutting Love's dividend
To make the quotient of Loss.

When the line was drawn beneath his calculations,
The book laid open for correction,
Too late he realised his great mistake.
At every stage, he had missed the point.

Fero City

(from *The Multiple City*)

Here no single person walks the streets.
You keep your personal guard close just
In case. Large dogs bound snarling, mean and cussed,
From alleys. Every pub has special seats
Where hard scarred men await their nightly treats,
The quarrel picked, the knife unsheathed, the thrust
That takes a life away, lays in the dust
A greenhorn tourist. Yes, folks, Fero City greets
The unwary. Yet, it seems, in many a flat
Short kindly women slice a Dundee cake,
Lay out the slippers, make their husband's tea,
And kiss him on the lobby's Welcome mat
With loving gaze, before he turns to make
Both hands and blade of all stains bright and free.

Feli City

(from *The Multiple City*)

Bliss in this city is put on display.
You need not look too far among the crowd
In every shopping mall, wherever loud
And mirthful voices rise from work or play,
Before you see a lighted face, a gay
Exalted smile. So many are endowed,
More than you think, with such a grace, allowed
By city fathers to have rights of way,
Rewards and medals, tax rebates. The mood
Of joy, the sigh of love, spills everywhere,
Softening the rain and breeze, zesting the food.
Relaxed convivial groups, a pair
Of lovers by the fountain, one man stood
In mystic rapture: common as pure air.

Tripli City

(from *The Multiple City*)

To this city come all things in threes.
Seated along the midden walls black craws
Croak to the bears at sprawling back-green ease,
While mice walk safe beneath their guide dog's paws.
Pert gleeful maidens, tripping home from school,
Throw each a coin into a fountain's spray.
The hungry wolf pursues a troika full
Of pigs; and keen stripped rivals face the fray.
Tall musketeers lounge at our Provost's door,
Twirling moustaches. Weird sisters crying "Hail!"
Accost tired East End sages and their store
Of gifts along a star-enlightened trail.
And, cooped up still in blessed virginity,
My love's French hens adore the Trinity.

Home Defence, 1943 [30]

Strange details surfacing from the mud
of decades. The weight mainly, too heavy
for a seven-year-old; the sling stiff
and tautened; wood dented and shiny.
Working the bolt needing a brother's
help, a whole hand's pressure
on the trigger for the click.
The only time I've ever aimed
a weapon of destruction.
.303 Lee-Enfield standard issue,
Home Guard, for the use of.
Left over, perhaps, from the last fracas,
retrieved from Passchendaele,
cleaned and re-cleaned respectfully.

Sighting out over a bedroom window-sill,
targeting an enemy advancing
across the field from Marchhill Drive
to storm the garden fence and
trample the shalotts.

Not noticing the foe already
occupying the high ground
in a father's throat.

Picnic

On this almost shortest day
the beach is empty, sun is low,
folding chairs from the Austin's boot
beside the driftwood seaweed fire

hold the parents. Three children
bulked in hooded parkas
kick a ball, pose with gull
feathers, heave at metal net-floats

by frayed blue and yellow nylon rope,
come running for Creamola,
cheese and ham on bakery bread.

The final act, to stand in line
before the coming tide along the voe
and innocently shout together,

"Happy New Year!"

Suicide

Why do I suddenly remember
Mr Whose Name I Have Forgotten?

Sitting at his own table
in the guest-house dining-room,

smiling at us students bantering
and punning in a pedantic group,

acknowledging Miss Whatsit's spinster
comments on his other side,

always in a suit, well-groomed,
probably retired from an office,

he had no life for us,
outside the breakfast and dinner hours.

Did we notice one day he wasn't there?
One evening he went into the sea

At Granton. I haven't thought about him
in fifty years. Logan, that was his name.

Mother

How attractive you are in these youthful photos
is always a surprise. School dux runner-up,
hockey-sticked, dark-haired, at times with glasses.

Not surprising that you fled the lochside village
finding a London life with bachelor girls on clerical grade
before the decade-long engagement ends with marriage vows.

Twenties flapper, thirties mother, forties widow.
Another effect of war. By day, efficient cheerful
Mrs Mac deploying her County Buildings phone

to move supplies of coal around the shire; by night,
a silent weeper in the single bed, fearful of shaming
bourgeois poverty, of being a burden.

Of course there were admirers. Once, having had me
dismiss an amorous dentist from the doorstep, you sighed,
I could secure our futures any day, but... – pausing –

compared with your father...... The rest unsaid.
What was it drove us apart from you, one son to uniforms
and Africa, the other to books and studies?

Possessive clinging, bizarre religion, a regiment of women?
In these long latter years too much separation,
too much silence, spiky relationships with sons and wives.

Still, at the end, no fuss, no trouble to others.
The sudden heart attack by night, a quick departure,
 not much to clear out from the small flat. Yet now,

though direct memories fade down twenty years,
your potted African violets put out again and yet again
their bright collateral abundance.

Passing Places

Haven't you noticed recently we are beset on every side
By life's non sequiturs as coming through the lochside birches
Thinking them silver ghosts of past decisions thronging in our path
Pushing their separate spreads of arrowheaded leaves to fall and grow
Again year after sodden year to touch us only in their clinging on to boots
And trouser legs for moments till they fall upon the metalled single-track
Sheep-droppinged road back to our car and thermos flask we then find
They come with us unnoticed down the road map to the city street plan
And the oil-stained garage floor floating from rucksacks anoraks
Damp socks to pierce a shadow of a conscience with memories of snow
On hills a sun transfiguring the wind chill factor to exhilaration and a glint
Of welcomed pain did we not then upon the home straight run that brings
The pension and the bus pass know of course the kidding has to stop
Of course the knee gives trouble and the mirror every day sniggers
At what it sees but whatthehell pick up the birch blades press them
In the photo album and a leather book of all the poems that have lit
Your life since that electric shock that switched your youth to on
Turning the volume up to max the colour to full bright and contrast
Keep them then upon the bedside table beside the glass of water
And the final tablets.

Immemoriam

It is true what MacDiarmid said we must reconcile ourselves to the stones
Every one I rake out of the border every chip of gravel on my path will be here
Long after me and mine all the war memorials with the names of uncles
Trim flat gravestone in the cemetery beside the firth a misspelt marker
Near the ruined ivied lochside church the church itself all these outlive the flesh
And blood our kin of past and future passing growths upon a silicate reality
Which in its turn sheds all shapes and scratches we impose returning to a basic
Stoneness waiting patient and implacable for the next turn of geological fashion
So what to do about the evaporating generations a grandfather now living only
In the memories of two ageing brothers his churches stand unmindful of their
Builder a grandmother who saw Mr Gladstone speak and counted a hundred
Gaelic birthdays the family from the glen cleared to a barren island a trusting
Clansman who followed his chief and bought it on Culloden field his cousins
Sent indentured to make another's profit in the Carolinas all our nameless kin
Invisibly remote under the enduring hills can there be monuments gravestones
Plaques and cairns to every modest local punter sufficient to push back
Forgetfulness into another eyeblink century as we carve out names we see
Already how time's scouring fingertips pick at the crisp incisions and a breeze
Through the corrie bears the first flakes out to new beaches of immortal sand.

Where Have You Sprung From?

It is a lottery for all the kings and their sad consorts
making dynastic plans, the block, the battle, dangerous labours,
bleeding sickness and the plots of cousins frustrate the hopes
of history, did we expect it would pan out, come at any point
to be otherwise, I ask you in all the cynical awareness of a media
analyst, Fortune turns her weighted wheel and the ball clicks
effortlessly into the red not black, the croupier slides the half-expected
deuce to banjax expectations, the row of pineapples in the bandit's
window does not come round, the arrow does not miss the eye,
the stupid preachers do persuade the seasoned warmen to rush
down the hill, it is a false pregnancy for the desperate queen,
why do I concern myself with these cut-outs of the past, the might-
have-beens of an exploded historicism, who cares about the sneering
bearded regents, proud kinsmen taking the gold of alien monarchs,
it's the economy, stupid, follow the money, where did the harvests go,
look at the cost of living, the wages spiral, shifting patterns
of a northern climate, lead in the water, arsenic in the creams,
stands Caledonia wild and woolly, sits she on her stern, lies she
with her martial cloak, don't ask me pal I'm just here for the beer
am I right or a meringue aye you're right you're an empire biscuit.

Pictures in an Exhibition

(With appropriate Russian music)

Time to take another turn around the gallery.
The curator greets you with a knowing wink.
Look, there are new exhibits along there at the end.
All in good time. You'll get to them.

Yes, these early ones are much as you remember,
Though the background music's mood
Has gained a darker tone. The smiling infant
At the garden gate beside the apple-tree,

The tired-eyed mother and the vanished father's
Vacant space, a kilted pose on the beached
Rowboat's bow, the shuttered summerhouse
In the long grass of a lost domain. A promenading

Theme escorts you into the adjoining room.
Period groups — impressions of the smoky bar, punts
On the river, marriage a la mode, the social
Whirl. Wild surreal notes accompany a style

That dominates the later rooms. Fractured faces,
A touch of Guernica in a Dutch interior,
Some abstracts, overstated colour blocks,
After Pollock, Hopperesque . What is the artist, the composer,

Saying? Gone the fiddles and the flutes?
Do you detect a note too brassy, a mood too minor
In the crisp toccata? Why the blurred features,
The empty swimming-pools, those black black

Crows above the contorted trees? You note
The imposing space there at the end, reserved no doubt
For a final canvas. Should we envision
A Great Gate of Kiev, exit in crescendo,

Tutti, fortissimo, blowing, banging, scraping
Fit to bust, colours merging into white light?
Or will it be like too much else, self-conscious edging
Off and through the overlooked side-door,

Out, out into the undistinguished passing day?

The Picture of Doreen Gray

Darlings, wasn't it awful about Doreen?
She'd gone completely gaga at the end,
Apparently. The mess in her flat, the parties,
Music, wild dancing, all the rest. They had
To break the door down finally,
The neighbours insisted. And what they found,
Champagne bottles, broken glasses, caviare
Trodden on the parquet floors, lines of coke
Upon the marble tops, a trail of Janet Reger
Leading to the circular bed, black sheets
All stained and crumpled. That Italian Adonis
She'd taken in, he was there, out for the count,
His sweet sun-tanned rump saluting the day.
And Doreen? In the jacuzzi, would you believe,
Wearing a smile and all her pearls. Golden hair,
Long, loose and damp. Dead, dead,
Never to spit another gutter oath or kiss
Another Ivan or Olga. Nevermore.
Her heart, they said. A miracle it hadn't happened
Years before.

But here's the truly funny thing. Something
To make you frown and scratch your heads.
Among her treasures, all the sculptures, all
The paintings round the Art Nouveau interiors,
One portrait hung in pride of place —
A sweet old lady, blue-rinsed, spectacled,
Very Queen Mum, holding her knitting,
Smile you wish your granny'd given you
Offering the bag of pandrops. Could have been
Doreen. In another life, same features,
Eyes and nose, too old, of course, must
Have been eighty, ninety, if a day.
Her nan, her mum? Who knows, perhaps,
When did sleazy untamed Doreen the Bad
First slink into our crazy party scene?
Way before our time, that's sure.
Gives you a frisson, touch of the shudders,
Just to think about it. Not to be dwelt on,
Darlings. Refill, anyone?

The Nth Dr Who

Look, I am back again
With my blue tumbling spinning box
And my radiophonic music
In one more regenerated form.
You have had the nutty professors,
Edwardian dandies, circus clowns,
The bright-eyed japesters and the
Fascinating hunks,
Looking out the narrow door
On yet another monster bash.
What will it be this time?
A new style-icon messiah for
The Saturday slot?

Think again.
You have but mistaken me all this while;
I have been and am yet
The Lord of Time.
I was with you as a child,
And I shall be with you at the end.
Coming before and after and beyond,
Charged with the darkest matter,
I walk in eternity.

In my last and highest avatar,
I shall return,
Sonic screwdriver burnished gold,
The wonky Tardis sorted,
Long coat and floppy hat reproofed
For the mental fight;
And that apocalypse will see
The final purge of your true demons,
Corporate enslaving cybermen,
Fanatical bomb-bearing daleks,
The spirit-sucking Beings from the Books
Behind them all.

However.... Are you ready for this?
I shall be requiring a companion.
Come from behind that sofa.

Hotel C'est La Vie

There is a problem with the keycard;
A supercilious porter comes to show you
How to enter, sneers at your luggage.

It turns out not to be the superior room
You were led to expect, only one chair,
No soft bathrobe, a back-street view.

Too late by now for the congenial dining-room.
Room service takes its time, the menu
Much less extensive than you hoped.

Down to suss out the bar. Pricey foreign beer;
A tired-eyed lady smiles an invitation
Across her Perrier, but not in fact to you.

Upstairs again, what madcap revels beckon?
Itemised temptations of the mini-bar,
Porn a la mode on the hotel channel,
Gideon Bible pristine in its drawer.

Lying in dark, you eavesdrop on the jungle.
Whispered quarrel in the corridor,
Sirens and slamming doors, insistent
Bleak transactions of the night.

Gasps and thumping headboard through the wall,
Machines and music of nocturnal tribes,
Fading at last into their pre-dawn stupor.

Would it could end in other than a slow awakening,
The light through the curtain chink, the paper
Outside the door, your morning call to Groundhog Day.

Rather a bursting open of the walls, sun
To pour light's cataract upon a new-made earth,
Your checking-out into a resurrection.

New Purchase

It was strange to see,
once I had got it home,
how all its colours brightened,

the angles rounded out,
the lettering sharpened,
almost as if it knew

this was its rightful home,
and I the destined owner.
Now it sits upon my desk

between the tray of pencils
and the usual coffee mug,
self-contained and tranquil.

It sparkles pleasurably
when I pick it up,
touch its shine, or on occasion

talk to it. Some recent evenings
I have noticed that it, half-
expectantly, turns toward me.

Back Gardening by Numbers

One Buddha on my patio step
beams back at the sun. Two black
cat-silhouettes patrol beside the buddleia
by four unmarked cat graves.
Three ceramic ducks frequent
the scallop-shells and primroses
upon the single grey-brick
planting feature. One famished fox
grubs deep for roots and
deconstructs one pigeon on the paving
into a thousand feathers
under the uncountable stars.

The Rake

You called me an old rake
in casual good humour,
and I thought, yeah,
that's not so bad.
An old rake
still keeps busy
gathering in spring blossoms,
rose petals of summer,
a glory of autumn leaves.
Applied with vigour,
it brings on the young grass.
Nobody throws away an old rake.
It just goes on
lounging around gardens
displaying its worn buffed sheen.
Let's hear it for old rakes,
scraping along through life.

From a Distance

Listen, you must understand these things aright.
The mountains have many silent reasons.
The deer follow their clear agenda.
The sea's discourse is moved by the moon's philosophies.
No arguments bend the grasses' firm resolve.

Under the sun the rain clouds neither go nor come;
'From' and 'to' have no meaning
Where no observer is defined.

What you were and are and will be
Are no more
Than a stirring of air over the water,
A flicker of light on the rock,
A shadow on the drying sand at the ebb.

However, this is no reason
to be depressed.

The Right One

The one who drove at you
    direct on the single-track road,
      he was not the one.

The one who turns on you
    at the bar-counter with an empty glass,
      he is not the one.

The one who will knock on your door
    with a briefcase of official papers,
      he will not be the one.

The one who may cling to you
    late at night in the hotel corridor,
      she may not be the one.

The ones who would serenade you
    unexpectedly at your birthday bash,
      they would definitely not be the ones.

You can know the right one
    in a number of unforetold ways
      that you will immediately recognise;

You may be tempted to laugh,
    but we do not advise it.

Rationalisation

mornings
it has been announced
will from now on
follow afternoons
which in their turn
will directly precede
nights
evenings will find a new slot
hosting the dawn
phonein show
immediately after
the dusk
spectacular
initially consumers
may experience some
dislocation of services
but with a degree
of goodwill
problems should be
quickly ironed out
and a new day
will have arrived

Statues

What is it about statues?

In all the capitals
they shout and puff
with strident equestrian triumph
—bronze Peter by the Neva,
Alfonso in the Retiro,
Jose in the Comercio,
eagled Wilhelm on the Rhine —
all the pompous emperors
in their magniloquent poses.

Give me instead three others
who blow these pretensions to the wind
- iron Cromwell beside the Parliament
he saved and broke,
eagle-beaked Wellington in Glasgow
wearing his traffic cone with pride,
and, best of all, the one I passed
each morning on the way to school,
no horse, no sword,
only the hodden grey,
the mouse, the flower,
a man as man,
the independent mind.

Polite Request

Remind these tearaway emotions
of their manners,
not to spill their wild hair
willy-nilly across our tidy desks,
not to shout their raucous
demands across the Sunday
luncheon table, and certainly
not to shoulder their way
into our decorous bedrooms,
laughing and crying
at their blatant joys and griefs
while honest folks are
trying to sleep.

Fabliau [31]

En été, le chat....
I sit in my solar and peruse
My lord's rich Book of Hours.
The peasants make their hay,
Birds fly in bluest skies,
Hills and fields gleam in opulent green.
I raise my eyes and look across
The same colours in my lord's demesne.
The procession on the page is matched
By that below. Sieur Tibert has come
To court me with his feline grace.
*Lady, I am assured your lord's body
Was observed with a Saracen arrow in the throat
Upon the wall of Acre. Time to choose.*

Sieur, I falter, *I must forbear deciding.
My vows of loyalty and chastity
Still bind me. In token I do wear this belt,
Which my lord fastened. Only he releases me.
Come, inspect it for yourself.*
Tibert gives his cat-smile and departs,
While young Squire Leo blushes to his golden roots.

En automne, le goupil....
Bright sun shafts on my bower walls.
I turn a page in the Book of Hours
And see the harvest fields aglow in gilt,
Hunters return with nets and spears,
The festival of ale and turning spit.
A cavalcade of knights and ladies winds
Towards a white-walled castle.
The Seigneur Reynard brings his subtlety
To woo in foxy style. *Lady, I bring you grief.
My lances late returned from Prussia
Report your lord's dead face espied beneath the ice
Of a Livonian lake. Accept the comfort
Of a hopeful friend.*

Seigneur, I say, *you grieve and honour me
In one. And yet the belt I wear to keep
My lord's faith and priceless jewel bright
And clean forbids accepting. Test it if you will.*

Lord Reynard's muzzle dips, and Lady Ange
Comes forward. Her hand is warm and lingers.

En hiver, le loup....
I huddle in my furs, crouch beside the fire,
Peer in a dim day's light upon my Book of Hours.
Black bare trees rise from white drifts,
Clouds on the hill, skaters on the pond,
Corpse on the gallows. Crossbows,
Pikes and hauberks, ladies in grey.
Who but the Baron Isengrim paying his wolfish call?
Lady, this coyness does your lord no credit.
I have it on report, three months gone,
He screamed for water, shrivelling in a cage
Slung from the walls of Chateau Mortfoi.
Such things can happen anywhere.

My Lord, I make reply, *I read your mind.*
I would oblige you, but I fear this burden
Laid upon me by a jealous lord has turned
Into my cross. Let your ladies prove with eyes
And hands the foul corruption
That consumes me. Indeed the Abbess Marguerite
Confirms the truth. A snarling Isengrim does then
Depart. I remember still the Abbess' touch,
Cool and firm..... and understanding.

En printemps, le joie de vivre....
Blossom on the cherry, oxen at the plough,
Pipes for village dancing, cuckoo on the bough.
I put my Book of Hours aside,
And, leaning over castle walls, I scent a new season.
A fresh wind spreads my hair.
Lady Ange, my new best friend, waits in our chamber.
She holds my gifts from Abbess Marguerite,
The device for women's easement
Favoured by the Sisterhood,
And a most ingenious key
Unlocking any man-made barriers.
Who knows, perhaps today
Blushing Squire Leo will again return,
Bringing a gift and message from his master,
Yet none more welcome than himself?

The Last Stories of Kilgore Trout [32]

(Kurt Vonnegut, Jr, American writer and satirist, died 12 April 2007)

Sat beside this old guy on the bus.
Got talking.
He told me about a country that was the richest land
On earth.
Inside it there were lots of other countries.
There was a native country,
And a black country,
And especially there was a country of poor people
And a country of sick people.
The native country had been robbed of its land;
The black country had been robbed of its language and culture.
The poor people's country was kept poor
And the sick people's country was kept sick
Because the rich and healthy people
Were Christians
And thought the poor and the sick were blessed
in their poverty and sickness.
So it goes, the old guy said.

Saw this old guy again yesterday.
Sat beside him again.
He told me a story
About a country that believed
In life, liberty and the pursuit of happiness.
Because of this they took away
The lives of thousands of people in other countries
With bombs and missiles and helicopter gunships,
The liberty of hundreds of people
by shipping them to a special prison
and chaining them up in tiny cells,
and the happiness of millions of people
by trying to give them democracy
and a market economy.
So it goes.

Met the old guy this morning.
Getting pretty tired of his stories.
But he told me another one.
There's this country that gives off
More poisons into the air
Than anywhere else on the earth,
And pays its scientists and politicians
To say that the world is safe in its hands.
So it goes, says the guy.

OK, I says,
What is this country?
The home of the brave
And the land of the free,
Says the old guy,
With all thy faults I love thee still.
It is my fate to tell these stories
And find them turned
Into pornography,
Or, even worse,
Science fiction.
So it goes.
Ting-a-ling.

Glasgow Beasts 2: The Next Incarnation [33]

(In gratitude tae ian hamilton finlay fur aa his braw stanes and gairden no tae mention his grett wee buik aboot the beasts and ither craturs o glesca)

wance
ah wis Pudgy
a budgie
fell doon thi cludgie
cam oot aw sludgy
pit inna boax
an sellt fur fudgie

\---------------------

aye
see me noo
ahm yir urban fox
Mister Cool
useti live it up
aff yir binbags
noo yiv blawn it
fuck thay wheeliebins
ferr warnin
kill yir pussy
fah get thi chance

\---------------------

here ah go
bizzin
    up
      an
        doon
ma wee ladder
rinnin
    alang
      thi
        plastic
          tunnels
buryin masel
in thi straw
wee Hammy
awways on thi move
happy as larry
dae wioot
this dinky gers strip
though

\------------------

back again
folks
here tae haunt yir
bourgeois
sensibilities
quiet wurd
fae thi teacher
get bizzy wi thi kame
an thi malathion
cheeky
wee bugger
o a heid louse
nits tae yous
pals
----
jings
ma no thi jinkies
fancy
        black
              nblue
                   shellsuit
white teeshirt
real posh
lotsa
attitude
me nma pals
gang aboot
in perrs
kick
thi shite
oota
aw yous burdz
say this
jist
wance
magpies rool
this
oor park
noo
----

nae fun
here
ah tell yi
tenth flerr
up in
Springburn
sittin
in thi bath
eatin tins a
dug meat
bitty kebab
time tae time
scarin thi wifie
no daen hir bizness
wan days end
tae thi ither
waitin
fur hir man
tae cowp me
in thi canal
see yi later
alligator
----

nae mair
nor five feet
fae me
at ony time
they say
less nor that in yir
braw
Clydeside
development
listen
dae yi hear me
waitin
its Jimmy Rat
by thi way
----

wee
grey
fella
on yir carpet
haw
no ootside
onna nicht like this
fa curl up
smaa
roon ma lotsa legs
pretend
ahm no here
jist a slater
fix yi
a guid
new suit
fyi like
----

ah sez
tae Jinty
zis no stupit
walkin
    up
       ndoon
george squerr
bobbin
ma heid
back
     nfurrit
jist fur sum
flaky crumbs
affana
Greggs bridie
cmoan kid
lets
   soar
      fur
        peace

Brian Splendid [34]

(i.m. Brian Osborne, 1941-2008)

You have the power to astonish us,
The scholarship, the dedication, all
Your talents serving to admonish us
Life's not a track to rest upon or crawl

Along unpurposed. You make firm new roads
On Scotland's map, enrich our place and time
With learning. How your laughing voice explodes
Mere words on pages to their just sublime.

See those mountains, the Munros you've scaled;
Many will follow up the paths you've conned.
You've tramped and climbed, your spirit has prevailed.
Your world is vast, in Scotland and beyond.

Fitting your grave should mark, in modest state,
The silk highway to Samarkand's lost gate.

Changing Guard

They're changing guard at Buckingham Palace —
Christopher Robin went down with Alice.
Police with guns were everywhere,
"They're here to make us safe, my dear,"
      Says Alice.

They went down to the Underground —
Two men in jeans said, "You terrorist hound."
They put six shots into Christopher's head,
"My goodness, dear, I think you're dead,"
      Says Alice.

The inquest found he had it coming —
He was clearly planning a suicide bombing.
His bear was suspiciously brown in hue,
"I never did trust that Winnie the Pooh,"
      Says Alice.

Alphabeat 35

All that jazz
Blows me away,
Cornet and sax
Dreamy and low.

Easy beat and rev,
Feeling *déjà vu*
Gets me in the gut,
Heart-thump sounds
In the inner ear.

Jack's back from Iraq,
Keeps rhythm in his cap,
Loves how its brio
Makes his music heaven.

Norma and Pam from Birmingham
Open their song so casual,
Picking the chords with a dainty flick,
Quite astounding the club DJ.

Rockin' and rollin' Tutti Frutti,
Shakin' and quakin' through and through,
Takes us back to the oldtime swinging
Under the mirrorball's shimmering stuff,
Very Sixties, love and peace.

Would you come and hold my hand,
Xena, my warrior princess chic,
Yodelling clear as I stand dumb,
Zealously guarding our love's etcetera?

Haibun – To The Deep North [36]

Why to the north? Those cliffs of ice, crevasses deep as Niflheim, the men in furs. Can that sea carry me over to the land of white expressionless bears, women with cheeks of fire who welcome strangers to their snow-house hearths?

Standing under the winter sun beside my garden pots, I see no further than these low besprinkled hills. Beyond, I imagine grey unsettling seas, gull-excited isles, weedy washed rocks of grief.

The narrow road to the deep north is one for mystics, poets, sages with bare feet and shaven heads. I re-enter my heated kitchen.

the Pole Star
draws the worthy traveller
beyond the comfort zone

Cunning Plan for Honourable Victory

Our wise all-powerful Shogun has decreed
his wooden Castle of Sudoku by the Eastern Sea
with its nine floors and eighty-one rooms

shall be held equally by the nine clans
of the Mountain Confederacy,
none holding pre-eminence.

The daimyo of each clan shall sit in the Presence Chamber
to receive audience and pronounce
the ineffable justice of the Shogun.

Two scholars, a sage and a poet,
shall share a study, to dispute the classics
and compose innumerable haiku.

The three wives of the daimyo shall occupy
a special apartment with thickened walls,
lest their bickering disturb the castle's order.

Four honourable sons of the lord shall learn
the arts of war and governance
within the Hall of Preparation.

The five sweepers and cleaners
shall, in their few hours of respite,
bed and refresh themselves in a plain dormitory.

The six best shamisen players of the clan
shall practise and perform their music
in the Salon of Ever-Open Windows.

Seven samurai (of course) shall hold
themselves in martial readiness
in the fully-equipped Guardroom.

For the delectation of the daimyo's family
and senior retainers, eight courtesans
shall provide tea and services in the Temple of Pleasure.

Cooks and noodle-makers (to the count of nine)
shall cater to the clan abundantly
in the Grand Refectory.

When the black ships of the blue-eyed foreigners
sail (as they must) into the eastern bay,
the Shogun's ultimate plan of subversion

by mental torture in the three stages
of Mild, Difficult and Fiendish
shall encompass the foreigners' downfall.

A cognate strategy will be employed at the Castle of Karaoke.

Eclogue – In The Gallery [37]

(Two Glasgow art-connoisseurs find themselves sharing the same tastes before a large canvas.)

He. Come lunch with me and be my love
And we shall all the pleasures prove
That well-fed lust may importune
Through the impassioned afternoon.

She. I'd lunch with you, but as to love,
We need to see what food may move
Libido to a sprightly tune.
Too well-fed lust kills passion soon.

He. I see you find this art-sex merry-go-round
A thoroughly familiar stamping-ground.
She. Art and sex are always in conjunction
And lunch has a vital linking function.

He. Let it be neat and light, as you well say;
Rogano does a crisp chilled Chardonnay.
She. Oysters perhaps, a croque monsieur,
A touch of salad, lightly dressed, demure.

He. Your taste's impeccable, a gourmet meal;
Art flatters Eros, do we have a deal?
She. If you provide this treasure trove,
I'll lunch with you and be your love.

Intelligent Design

Out in the deeps of the cosmos,
Where the galaxies wheel and grow,
The novas explode, dark clouds collide
And in chaos ebb and flow.
>   *But hum this catchy tune, folks,*
>   *Everything is fine,*
>   *It's all just part of a mighty plan*
>   *— Intelligent design.*

Some planets are gas, some planets are rock,
Their moons are dust or ice,
The rings are fragments of broken worlds,
The weather is not at all nice.
>   *But snap your fingers to the rhythm, folks,*
>   *This is the party line,*
>   *All that is made is very good,*
>   *— Intelligent design.*

The rocks are filled with fossils,
The species rise and fall,
Mammoths and dinosaurs self-destruct,
Neanderthals go to the wall.
>   *But chant these words of truth, folks,*
>   *There ain't no need to repine,*
>   *God's in His heaven, all's right with the world,*
>   *— Intelligent design.*

And here we are upon this earth,
The challenged in body and mind,
With TB and leprosy, Alzheimer's, AIDS,
And cancers of every kind.
>   *So sing out the triumph hymn, folks,*
>   *You're first in the glorious line,*
>   *Made in His image, the heirs to His bliss,*
>   *— Intelligent design.*

Endangered Species

Having surveyed the public rooms,
Central Hall and Dining-Room
(table laid in permanent anticipation
of Victorian guests in evening fig),
Library and sunfilled Morning-Room,
passing the jovial chatelaine in Barbour gilet
checking a mental abacus for each admission,
the paying visitors tumble down
servants' twisty stairs to where the Tea-Room,
blest terminus of outings,
provides them trays of cappuccinos, fruity scones
and jam to carry terracewards.

There the real purpose of the day
reveals itself. Along the balustrade,
perched on lichened busts and urns,
the boldest hopping on the picnic tables,
your clients and petitioners await –
chaffinches and sparrows, a single
blackbird, bullfinches to the fore –
the population of the formal garden
most disrespectfully request
your crumbs and currants, fragments
of your krispie crunch, the shortbread
with its millionairish topping.
They will pose for photo-ops,
should you desire them, give you the cheeky
birdie business, but do not be fooled.

Worms and grubs and slugs
all have their place, and so do you.
On all sunny, grey or rainy days,
April through October, ten till five,
you are the catering solution, meals on wheels;
so many calories an hour to stoke
the quick invisible wings, the hot blood's race,
against the undeferrable travel date,
the desperate pecking at the frozen earth,
the unlit eye, the rigid legs
                        below the ice-hung twig.

Small Stage

As in the smallest theatres
the actors and the audience
maintain their distance, exercise
their appreciated functions easily
across a gulf a metre wide,

so at this table, theatre of ritual,
you perform
looking at not seeing
me, I listen smile applaud,
the script interpreted revealing
its fullest nuanced passioned meaning,

and it is only later, having left
that brief arena of persuasion and belief,
the critic kicks in: what was that all about?

Planetary Response

("It is a paltry business to try to drag down the arduus furor of the stones to the futile imaginings of men...", from "On a Raised Beach", Hugh MacDiarmid)

I suppose I should be grateful
for your (recently discovered) concern
regarding my well-being, flattered indeed
by your wish to save me from catastrophe.

Your loudly expressed wishes to protect
and preserve my tigers, my elephants,
my whales, my layers and my sheets,
my everything, it seems, (except my rats and fleas)

have all been noted. Do I commend them?
Up to a point, my *homo sapiens*.
I have no memory of similar campaigns
on behalf of my trilobites, my dinosaurs,

my mammoths. Take my sea, for instance,
my shifting plates. It grows, it shrinks;
they come and go. I am still here.
The need for my salvation is not an issue.

Perhaps you misread our situations. I notice
how you change appearance with my seasons:
summer flimsies, floating fabrics; winter wools
and fleeces. So it is with me.

My lofty parent-patron who holds me
in his grip (the sun to you)
dictates what I shall wear – a suit of water,
hat of ice, coat of air and cloud, shirts

of grass and forest. I shift and change them
as required by flares and wind and solar messages.
Thus you too, my parasite populations,
water-dependent organisms,

have your good and bad days.
To me, *cela ne fait rien.*
The me that you ignore – that rock
and magma, iron core, the one essential Stone –
is unperturbed. Scratch and bore like mites,
gnaw and consume, make holes like moths,
ruffle my garments, then, in a panic
at the unaccustomed draught, preach

your sermons of salvation.
Forgive me if I stay unimpressed.
I shall merely adjust my dress,
O my bacteria, my Ephemeridae.

By the Way

It was an incidentally observed phenomenon.

The third satellite
Of one minor star
Showed slight irregularity
In the fluctuations
Of its surface temperature,

Indicated by a rapid shrinkage
Of its polar ice-caps.
We must deduce some attendant
Changes in the distribution
Of its water-dependent
Organic structures.

There was no visible explanation,
And, for an accredited observer,
Only the briefest note
Would have sufficed.

As it was, the situation
Rectified itself within a brief cycle
Of solar activity,
A few million or so
Planetary orbits.

Of much greater consequence
Is the impending arrival
In that galactic sector
Of the Dark Matter Cloud
That promises a fine spectacle
Of stellar conflagrations.

Its progress is being eagerly charted
By fireworks lovers
Throughout the cosmos.

The Falling Apartness of Things [38]

Finally it all goes pear-shaped,
Ultimately things fall apart.

You may think you have it safely taped,
the crisp initials in the diary,
shirts all colour-coded in the wardrobe,
all the empties out in the recycling bin
—until it starts to slip and
lose its focus. The spider scuttles across
the carpet; the TV screen implodes
upon Big Brother; and that
blue insipid fluid drips from every tap.

Was it for this you stood in line
for capping by the Chancellor,
made all the monthly payments to the Pru,
employed those nubile babysitters to canoodle
with their boyfriends on your leather couch,
and watched your house price yo-yo
as your neighbours came and went?

I think not.

There is still time
    to bring the burly minder back from
                        his pampas exile,
    to fetch the locked box with its well-wrapped
                        contents down from the attic,
    to call the unlisted helpline on the green phone
                        in the linen cupboard,
    and scrape the coaldust off the trapdoor in the
                                cellar floor.

And then, just wait.

larus argentatus: the herring gull

the saga of fnc gull

the opinions and emissions of fnc gull, larus argentatus

I *In which our hero introduces himself in all his raucous egotism*

aye its me sunshine here at yir windae
tap tappin who did yi think it wis
poes fukin raven nevermore[1] lift yir heid
yi eejit tak pity oan an auld fowl of the air
jist passin by oan the road tae damnation
howsabout a bitty breid an cheese
mibbe some pickle or peanut butter
fair stervin oot here in the cauld
caw this bluidy may december mair like
you some kinna poet sitting at yir pc
aw warm an cosy zat yir study yir in
real soothside posh sandstone eh
caad on a poet yince oot anniesland wey[2]
he niver hid ony computer auld typeriter
suited him real gent wrote a poem
aboot me an my cauld eye fair chuffed
i wis aw come oan be a pal
if i can help someboady as i pass along
whaurs yir christian charity auld yin
ive just come doon fae the isle a skye
no verra big but im helluva sly
wanti hear a story sing fur ma supper
if yi like
                            jist the ither day
i wis sittin oan a bollard
up at oban pier mindin ma ain business
hid ma eye oan a coupla tourists
eatin fishn chips ooty a poke alang
comes a wee runt ae a traffic warden
lookin fur business seein if he could
catch a caur or two on the double yellas
sees me an swings his fist in the air
sayin get oota it or avaunt and quit my sight[3]
or some sich discourtesy no takin that
fae onybody lazily flaps aff the bollard
does a graceful swing roon the harbour
comes roon again to whaur hes pit
his wee computer thingie on a caur roof tae
note the number and print his wee ticket
then splat i gets him full on his baw heid
splashin his machine and gettin the shiny

car roof wi the same payload splat jist like that
moments lik yon mak it aw worthwhile
thats ma kinna poetry write ma odes an epics
on aw the noble works ae man splat
fnc gull wis here.

thats me by the way
fnc gull
they ken him here they ken him there[4]
yon effin seagulls everywhere
seriously strong cheddar eh
and a daud ae branston yir a real pal
ill be back mak nae mistake
but nane ae that shitey marmite
or yir oot the windae
be seein ya

II *In which fnc gull deplores slanderous imputations*

hey big yin you in therr
sittin at yir desk i can see
yir minds no on the job kiddin
oan yir wurkin starin at the screen
thinkin yull hae a shot at playin
battleships this is me back then
jist lik i said fnc gull
remember dyi hiv ony ae that
cheese or some quatri formaggi
pizza goat a taste fur nosh
italiano ever since i stertit
hingin oot wia coupla tally gulls
fae the med wurkt thir wey
up here yin pizza parlour
n bistro eftir anither till they
goat tae glesca they baith
swear blin the best bitsa pizza
ur kebab they ever swallied
cam aff the pavements atween
the tron an charin cross carlings
n buckie were whit gave the real kick
naethin else lik it onywhere
in the eu see in the herald
by the way uz gulls is gettin
a bad name pesterin the guid
citizens in aw the touns airdrie
kilmarnock the big glesca
hoosin estates aw yon divebombin
the weans scatterin the middens
keechin the statues heids whit
a palaver blame uz fur aw the problems
scapegoatin the innocent avian
fraternity fur thir ain shittiness
effin liberty kin yi blame
a few fledgies fur lettin aff steam
i mind masel when i wis young
a richt bampot zoomaway
up in lerwick rerr time me n ma pals
usety hae rippin up the binbags
three or fower ae a bricht simmer moarn
skriechin fit tae bust waukin
aw the shelties n norski fishermen

tae their hamebroo hingowers
easy pickins then fishguts galore
mutton scraps hame bakin
aw cheynged noo probly lik
ivrywhere else wheelie bins
his ruined the gemm
tempora mutantur[5] auld yin
zat no richt nos et mutamur
in illis aha that foxed yi
didny expect a bitty the classical
jazz fae a scruff lik me didny
ken id spent some profitable
months roostin on the windae
ledge ae a major seat uv learnin
pickin up thi knowledge fur free
a plague a these pickled herrins[6]
the dominie said nae wey tae talk
tae a sober seafaring gull
left ma trademark oan his dusty
windypane splat double splat
goat the pizza hiv yi nice bitty
anchovy i see yir a pal
be oan ma wey then goat a big
contract up in tobermory
some fine pentit hooses[7] therr
waitin tae be signed aff in ma
ain inimitable fashion
see yi later

III   *In which fnc gull meditates on devolution and fraternal harmony*

its aw yin tae me big fella
devolution ur no naebody tells me
whit i canny dae reserved pooers
indeed loada shite ony blackbacked
bugger ur bonxie tryin tae pull wecht
sayin lay aff the trawlers ur the
chinkies dustbins thats ma patch
get his een peckt oot soon as look
dinny staun fur it i say readin
in the scotsman this moarnin therrs
a real posh eastcoastie rag
by the way it wis sayin some guy
wis pushin fur a british day[8]
tae bring the fowk ae these sceptred
isles closer thegither aw john thomsons
progeny yin happy family lik
ay thatll be richt spent a coupla
weeks last winter doon sooth
fur the sake ae ma health upn doon
the mighty thames auld faither t
hissel rollin along down tae the mighty sea
caa that a river noo the rhine
yons a river n a hauf onywey
therr wis i perched upon westminster bridge[9]
aye i ken earth hisny onythin
tae show mair polluted id say
fair choked oan aw thae fumes
up comes twa three cockney gulls
fulla shite n rhubarb wotcher jock
doon fae the snowy wastes ae jockland
heh heh strike me pink me owld
cock sparrow listen pal i says
lessa this cheeky chappie banter
can yi direct me tae yinna thon
internationally acclaimed jellied eel
stands i hae a notion tae sample
yir ethnic cuisine not so farst squire
wanny them says oo do you fink
you ahr swannin in ere as if
you owned the plice you jocks
dont belong ere sod off to your igloo

118

pardon me i says wir aw british
urnt we an this is oor capital
famed in song an story ownly if we
say so mac an were sayin oppit ah weel
i says i see that rational discourse
is up oan the slates an you nigels
is dur fur a lesson in political realities
need i say mair i think not
therrs a sairheidit gang ae yineyed
brakenwinged lari ridibundi
hirplin somewhaur aroon bow bells
ruein the day they tangled wi fnc gull
afore i left the big smoke i tuik
a turn aroon big ben an left ma callin card
wi the mither ae parliaments splat
ive been thinkin big fella see this
place yiv goat doonby at holyrood
dinny knock it sno sae bad
but yon boats up the roofll[10] no dae
no a net ur a bucket ae fishguts
tae be seen reminds me whaurs
yir manners hauf an oor ive been stood here
bletherin no a sign ae a piece
howsaboot some fish paste or a rollmop
yi need tae get oot mair doon tae waitrose
ur m n s thats real food
ah yir a pal so yi ur
see yi later

IV   *In which fnc gull discourses on sausages and football*

help ma boab auld yin whit a cairry-oan
naethin but crappy fitba evrywhere ye luik
as i said awready help ma boab jings
sorry fur the patter ive been owerdaein
ma perusal ae the sunday post
n ither cosmopolitan chip wrappins
this last wee while flappin owre dundee
an the mair deprived arrondissements
in glesca an the central belt
fitba yi can keep it sez fnc gull fur yin
see this world cup palaver[11]
utter keech if yill pardon ma french
i wis doon in gerryland drinkin the waters
when it wis gaun oan see thae gerry
sausages by the way best ive evir
sampled no the wurst at aw heh heh
get them mit zwiebel jawohl mein herr
wia bitty onion tae yous monoglots
an some mustard pure wagner
onywey the way i see it this fitbaz jist
an incitement tae aw thatz ridiculous
fat baldy guys gaun mental
at a bunch ae expensive poseurs
batterin a wee baw aboot a field
keepin the needy winged denizens ae the air
awa fae the worms an a medicinal dose
ae herbage needless to say
i expressed my displeasure
in the timehonoured way fae time tae time
usa splat ukraine splat
portugal v nigeland splat splat
france v italy splat splat splat
jules rimet cup direct hit splatter
splat oh the satisfaction oh the orgasmic
release ae pentup tensions as ive said
tae my therapist sigmund the auld bonxie
fae unst naethin lik a guid extrapolation
tae clear the physical an metaphorical tubes

an hes in fu accord though hes mair yin
fur batterin heids a behavioural response
ma pacifist principles dinnae haud wi izzat
a lorne sausage bap wi hp
i see in yir haun cmoan sees a daud
afore i depairt fur the benighted wastes
ae ibrox whaur i hear the auld firm
ae chancers n shelties ur due fur yit
anither titanic struggle i wish
tae add my siller haufcroons tae the general
mayhem splat oan yir hoops[12]
splat oan yir gers serve them richt
fur turnin the youth ae this fair city
awa fae the simple pleasures ae meccano
an stamp collectin see yi later
big fella up the jags sez fnc gull

V *In which our hero bids farewell (with a hint of later return)*

this is it auld pal
time fur offski fnc gull
sez au revoir we huvti stop
meetin lik this nae mair
ae thae draughty windae ledge
exchanges these proceedins ur closed[13]
as the big mac said speakin ae which
yi widnae hae a spare bitty
burger aboot yir person nae pressure
jist a thocht ah weel nae point
in lingerin ive hid ma fill
ae city life evri few months
when the wind turns tae the west
this notion comes upon me
tae see the hills an glens an shiny lochs
fae the best ae viewpoints
way way up a kye[14]
wee touch ae sentiment there
yill notice twa barely haudback
tears bedewin the cauld hard een
ae fnc the auld seafarer
spreader ae pithy sense n shite
oan scotias cloudy knowes[15]
ach but its nae sae bad
this wee place ae oors tae soar
abuin the aforesaid hills etc
san honour tae be treasured
see the richt kinna day yi can observe
the haill clanjamfrie[16] side tae side
sea tae shinin sea[17] breathes there
a gull i say and drap my benison
oan aw beneath ben nevis splat
loch rannoch an lochaber splat
schiehallion schiehallion[18] splat galore
an aw the meccas eldorados
culinary heavens tae be swoopt
upon in airborne ecstasy
loch fyne oyster bar the happy
haggis mctavishs kitchen
an aw the wondrous chippies
ae the gaidhealtachd[19]
fair maks ma guts rummle

jist thinkin aboot it yi widny
hae a battered fish wi ketchup
aw furget it i canny hing aboot
the sea is at the flood the cock
is at the craw an fnc gull
is oan the wing
bye bye the noo
fareweel an adieu tae yi
ladies ae spain bearsden
milngavie or giffnock
an aw yir weelstockt fridges
but as the big guy said
when aw seems lost
an totally fukd
i shall return[20]

the travels and further effusions of fnc gull
vagabond extraordinaire

I   *In which fnc gull returns with tales of travel*

heh big man you in therr
get yirsel ower tae yir
windae pronto cmoan
sconeface its me near deid
so i am fnc gull remember
yir wee pal the effin seagull
oh ay act aw surprised yi thocht
yid seen the last ae me aw thae
months syne nae sich luck
im back wia vengeance
swoopin fae the cloods
lik a pintsized valkyrie come
tae unload the wecht
ae retribution oan aw
evildoers splat no tae yir
guid sel uv course ma true
an ainly benefactor speakin ae
which whaurs the grub
im gaspin fur a hot dog
ah the quizzical gaze i see
yir wonderin why the wee guys
eftir a belt ae the transatlantic
junk nosh yill be wonderin
tae i guess in yir usual
beaky manner whit yir fnc
gulls been up tae aw thae
months aff oan the randan
wonder nae mair im here
tae tell yi ma deeds ae derringdo
ower the gret pond in the u s uv a
land ae the free an hame
ae the brave[21] weel maybes aye
maybes hooch aye therr i wiz
glidin awa fae this city ae sin
an shadow bound fir tir nan og[22]
ur maybe arran when splat kapow
i flees bang intae yinna thae
wind turbines theyre slingin up

aw ower the shop deathtraps
fur yir innocent avian
wayfarer as i said splat
next i kens im comin back
tae sense and sanity oan the deck
ae a ginormous container ship
left wing banjaxt bruise oan
ma heid the size ae a limpet
headache bangin lik a hielan
hingower at hogmanay an
heidin aff intae the settin sun
yons hoo i goat ma free
ticket tae the land ae the
big mac

tellyi mair next time im aff
fur ma supper seein yir no
comin up wi the goods
maybe pick up a single fish
doon the nearest chippie
try tae dae better pal packet
ae frankfurters wid gae doon
a treat hiv a nice day

II *In which our hero meets a formidable mademoiselle*

therr yi ur auld fella its yirsel
im back gulliver returns fae his travels
wi mony a tale tae tell whaur wis i
ah yes america ma new fund land[23]
heavin intae view an me oan the deck
testin ma wings tae see if theyd
wheech me aff tae fast food pastures
new felt lik a cheynge eftir aw yon
galley scraps hell ae a lotta curry
oan thae big boats cudnae luik
anither chapatti in the coupon
okay then sez fnc gull time tae declare
ma genius[24] an aff i flaps a wee touch
crooked an hivn tae correct the course
fae time tae time jings wis i oot
ae condition it wis aw i cud dae
tae mak a skittery landin oan the ear
ae this big stane lassie[25] staunin oan
a wee green island haudin up a
jumbo sized icecream cone
heh therr big jinty i sez whits
the best route fae here tae a guid deli
piss aff she replies petite merde
ae a oiseau scruff lik yous furrin
gulls isny wantit roon here ony merr
zut alors i sez whits aw this pardon
ma french cairryoan i thocht yi
wis real live auntie samantha[26] born
oan the fourth ae july nae fear she scoffs
zese stupide yankees zink i am wanny
zem yet i am pure francaise nestcepas
fer fae ma ain patrie la belle france
an noo vasten vite yir ruinin the
tourists pictures ae bonnie liberte
awa an report tae hameland security
richt then big wumman i sez
if this is hoo yi treat a puir wee
huddled mass[27] fae the ends
ae the earth im fur offski
but i left her sumpn fur the weekend
a wee dab ae the seagull number
five ahint her lug splat

ah fur petes sake jimmy ma belly
thinks ma throats cut hiv yi no
goat ony nourishin scraps yi want
recycled ah weel im aff tae yir trendy
local tapas bar i fair fancy
a wee daud ae chorizo bye fur noo

good on ya big man is aw this
fur me black puddin haggis balls
yiv goat a rerr insicht intae a gulls
secret passions an desires jist gies a wee
moment tae sample the goodies

aye whit wis i sayin the last time
i left yi hingin aboot in new york harbour
me pechin ma weary way fae big liberty
belle across tae manhattans topless towers[28]
fair desperate tae dive intae the fleshpots
an delis an burger stands ae the big aipple
oh whit a noble sicht did then unfold
alang the waterfront line upon line ae
noodle bars sushi an crispy beef an sweet
an sour an chow mein no furgettin the humble
burger an hot dog aw the treasures ae the orient
an beyond dinna mind ma slaverin aw owre
yir clean windae sill thats whit the usa
is aw aboot visible wealth an conspicuous
consumption adam smith[29] neer dreamt
the hauf ae it onyweys therr i wis really
gettin stuck intae the scraps and
throwaways when i hears a croaky voice
up above me heh doon therr im watchin yi
did ma wee hert near stap beatin wi fricht
honest auld fella i thocht ma days wis numbered
an hed come fur me at last times great black
backie wi the murderin beak an fnc gull
wis fur the last dive tae davy jones but then
i heard it again cmoan skinny beam us up
some tasty morsels i looks up an therr they
wur aw sittin row eftir row ae yankee gulls
but whit a gaitherin talk about laterally
challenged fower ae me wid fit intae yinnae
thon sumo monsters each wid tak up three
seats on the pier heid seems tae me pal
i sez yi cud dae wi layin aff the tasty morsels

help tae shed some ae thae surplus grams
yiv been pilin oan grams buster yinnae them
squawks whit unamerican talk is yon ur you
some kinna ayrab listen chubby i ripostes
watch ma beak hear ma dulcet tones scots
pal here oan a fleein visit fae the auld
country yi ken hoch ay ciamar a tha sibh[30]
wings across the sea an up i flaps tae jine
the heavy mob scotch eh the heid yin sez
come oan in an meet the faimly im big louie
by the way an aff he gaes intae a blast
ae his latest rap
listen to me mac im a tellin you straight
don't interrupt to remonstrate
im here to tell you that from today
youre a welcome guest in the usa
help yourself to the dogs and fries
and feed yourself to a proper size
dont stint on the pretzels the rye and pastrami
keep cramming down the wurst and salami
top it up with apple pie and strudel
thats how you become a true yankee doodle
aw very weel jimmy i interposes but hiv yous
lookt at yirsels lately yous kin scarcely flap
doon tae the nosh let alane get back up again
whit yous need is a guid personal trainer tae
get yiz back in shape an i herewith offer ma
professional services yir oan sez big louie
an thats hoo i fund ma first joab as an illegal
immigrant tell yi mair soon auld guy
im awa tae the landfill fur a bite

back again auld pal uryi sleepin ok thae nichts
yir lookin a wee thing peaky no takin yir horlicks
lik yi should ur maybe yir owredaein it
on the crabmeat fair unsettles the gut
even a hardy gull lik yirs truly his a wee
problem wi the crustaceae get tae yir bed
im sayin but no afore i tell yi hoo i cam tae leave
gods ain country an wing it fur hame
the joab as personal trainer tae big louies lot
didny pan oot as i hoped whit a useless lazy
shower ae greedy gluttons could i keep them
aff the snackin and the guzzlin no a chance
they kept oan pittin oan the flab nivir daein their
twice daily flichts oot ower the watter
across tae long island ur brooklyn no turnin oot
fur the charity sponsored wingathons an it wis
gettin tae me as weel owre easy tae let the schedule
slip and grab anither pile ae scoff fae the endless
free buffet ae the new york scene cam the day
big man when i tuik a reality check an fund i wis
jist becomin anither ae big louies lot in size and
habits thats it i sez im no fur here goodbyee cheerio
au revoir an aff i lumbered lang takeaff slow ascent
no easy i kin tell yi but there it wis nae handy big boat
this time aroon it hid tae be the scenic route
picture yir fnc gull sayin a last regretfu fareweel
tae the culinary glories splat an splat again
afore headin north alang new englands stern
an rockbound coast[31] a solitary pilgrim oan the
airways ae life made guid progress im gled tae
report gettin fitter by the day cuttin back
oan the grub feelin the wings gettin stranger
quite yir auld fnc gull eftir a week or twa
the fechtin spirit back wia vengeance saw aff
twathree rovin bands ae native american robber
gulls fell in at last wia a traivellin companion mair
tae ma peaceable tastes cheery gull fae maine caad
edgar makin his way hame eftir a big convention
in florida ainly drawback he wis keen

tae convert me tae the true path fur gulls yi see
effin hed say if yi jist follae the sayins ae jonathan
yir lifell turn aroon an aw will be hunkydory
it seems this jonathan wis some kinna supergull
wha hid the richt message
jonathan livingstone seagull[32]
way back in a gowden age ae love an peace
seemd a real wimp ae a gull tae me
but i didny argue edgar wis sae fu ae him
tell the truth i wis gettin fed up tae here with
the sainted jonathan hoo hed guide us through life
save us fae distress an tak us up tae his nest
in cloodiegullburgh[33] when we snufft it but it aw
endit when edgar disappeared fae his perch
oan a rock yin nicht nivir saw him again
jonathan must hiv cam fur him and wheeched
him aff didny tak his feathers though they were aw
spread aroon either jonathan or maybe fascinatin
mr fox i didny hing aboot tae check
goat on my way fast lik i said auld freend
yir no luikin that great awa tae yir bed
an ill jist clear up thae last wee scraps
ae black puddin ill be back suin tae cheer
yi up wi ma thochts on eternity mortality
an the utter shiteyness ae cheap air travel
nighty night

V   *In which fnc gull meditates on mortality, religion and beaches*

aye its great whit a guid nichts sleepll dae
fur yi yir luikin mair lik yir auld shabby
chic sel feelin lik a million dollars i trust
mair nor i wis feelin no lang eftir i stertit
the lang flicht back ower the northern seas
tae caledonia luve an beauty talk aboot the derk
nicht ae the soul believe yir fnc gull when he sez
he wis truly sadly deeply sunk in it
up tae his oxters an nae dawn in the eastern sky
i tell yi big man i wis close tae giein up the ghaist
naethin but grey sea and whitecaps horizon tae
bluidy horizon no a lot in the grub line either cam
doon tae settle time tae time adrift oan the bosom
ae the briny luikin fur shoals ae wee fish maistly
in vain i may say whaur hiv they aw gane seems
theyve duin a runner thats when i began tae regret
leavin new york an aw its riches canny relax
either sittin doon therr oan the surface
owre mony fearsum beasties lurking aneath
ready tae grab a toothsum wee gull wis i no
gled tae come across a coupla tankers and cargo
boats i wis able to slipstream
fur the odd day guddlin in their slops
an perchin oan their stickyup bits snuffin
the cauld atlantic airs goat tae thinkin
auld pal whit if edgar hid it richt eftir aw
an there wis a jonathan ready tae flap tae oor aid
an mak it aw come guid fur evir an a day
wid that no be a rerr turnup but then
i thocht bein an empirical kinna penseur
i canny see a scrap ae real proof ony where
lifes a teuch bugger an its a sair fecht
but its aw wiv goat zat no a fact big buddy
therrs nae cloodiegullburgh up in the big grey
yonder the gemms a bogey such wis the musins
ae fnc gull upon eternity when bingo
the shout gaes up land ho in a mainner
ae speakin an i kent the lang days journey

133

intae nicht[34] wis ower the distant peaks ae
scotia hid swam intae view an aw shall be weel
an aw manner ae things shall be weel[35] specially
in the grub line an sae i flappt aff oan the last leg
ae the roun trip leavin a generous tip fur ma lift
splatter splat first rule ae the hitchhikers guide
shaw yir appreciation tae the driver
an sae it wis gentle reader i fetcht up
oan the distant hebridean strand
odysseus gull the stormtost wanderer hame tae
claim his richtfu place wastit nae time i kin tell yi
crabs limpets an some bitsa deid sheep theres aye
guid pickins oan a western beach luik aroon chum
neist time yir walkin the dug by the sea yir average
tidelines a lesson in mortality an a guid thing tae
sez fnc gull mak the best ae it while yi can
trust me auld yin i hiv seen the future
an it is mince reminds me wid yi hae ony
ikea meatballs in yir capacious larder gae doon
a real treat they need a bitta gravy hooevir tae
help them oan the wey doon see yi later

VI   *In which our radical hero stands out against feudal oppression*

yon wis a rerr holiday jaunt comin hame
tae ma ain patch eftir aw ma tribulations
see the hielans wha needs the warm sooth
eftir aw the stravaigin roon the new warld
whit a relief tae be wingin it ower the native
heath hills an glens galore samplin the local
delicacies goat tae be carefu thae days aw the same
wee tip auld pal stick tae fresh roadkill if yi can fin it
best wi the tyremarks still oan it ony ither deid
thingies leave them alane some ae yon forelock
tuggin gamies hiv a nasty habit ae spikin them
wi a wee touch ae the deidlies aw in the cause
ae preservin the lairdies sportin fun fairs fair
sez fnc gull whas tae miss an occasional grouse
chick hors doeuvre ur a wee egg breakfast time
tae time anither thing owre mony hooray henries
wi purdeys³⁶ ready tae blast aff at onything fleean
but therr i wis soarin free when i fell in wi twa
bauld lads fae the kessock³⁷ up inverness wey goat
on fine aw scruff thegither thocht wed hae
a wee bit sport with the locals cam across this
gowden eagle makin his noble progress back
tae his faimly big hare gruppt in his talons aw
stuck up beak an romantic poseur hey therr
big budgie i sez the three uv us sniggerin fit
tae bust gonny gies a peck at yir bunny
big bummer totally ignores uz silent scorn
treatment cmoan tweetypie we repeats share an
share alike brithers ae the air an i maks a grab at
his denner lay aff my wabbit the eagle squawks
lay aff i say scruffy fellows weel that did it
we fair set aboot him upshot wis he hid tae drap
his prey an we had a rerr picnic oan the rocks
while he soared awa in heich dudgeon fair cheered
up ma day i can tell yi like tae see thae toffee nebs
fair pit oot tell yi anither funny thing happend tae me
oan ma jaunt passed owre a castle giein it a splat
oan principle cam upoan a bunch ae tweedies haen

a picnic aw kilts an peelywally knees i say cabbage
auld guy sez pass the cucumber sannies anither
cuppa the earl grey camilla howsaboot an organic bacon
buttie harry aha i thinks micht be some uppah cless
nosh heah flees doon tae hae a shufti cheeky wee
bitch ae a wumman wi a crooky stick waves me aff
no staunin fur that whips up a bit tae get a guid aim
then delivers ma coup de grace gets the auld biddy
splat oan her jaeger heidscarf tuk aff in the best
ae spirits leavin her thinkin we definately urnae amused
no much mair tae tell big yin goat back here
relieved tae be still in wan piece
lookt up ma freens uv course including yir guid
sel back in the usual routine bit ae scroungin
bit ae the chat an the crack lifes no sae bad
dinnae heed ma blacker ruminations
fnc gullz his sel yince mair
sae yill no mind me askin
whits fur supper
duck pate oan crackers
ah yir kiddin me
see yi soon

weve been here afore big lad
mind a year or so back i cam tae tak
ma fond fareweels yon wis whit stertit
fnc gull aff oan his epic jaunt tae the new
warld wi aw the ensuin palaver ive been
deavin yir senses wi richt then here i come
again chappin at yir windae no jist bummin
a bite ae elevenses though that wid no be
unwelcome tae yir ever stervin wee pal
goat ony venison sausages a wee reminder
ae ma hielan tour ach weel no tae bother
im jist fur tellin yi im aff
nae kiddin this is it
fareweel a lang fareweel[38]
tae aw the cheery scenes ae urban life
whaur yir gull aboot toon ruled the roost
dispensin wit an wisdom wia gay an
splatterdash abandon movin oan auld freend
thats whit im daein its aff doon the watter
ma purpose hauds tae flee ayont the sunset[39]
maybe owre the pond yince mair cud luik up
big louie and his pals see if theyre back in trim
louie wis tellin me aboot this place hed heard ae
nevir been there but it seemed a paradise fur gulls
frisco bay awa tae the furthest west
cud set ma sichts oan it maybe hitch a lift
no much merr tae be said big fella
its been a privilege pal this last while
jist yin last thing be ma witness
tae thae final wishes here goes

the last testament ae fnc gull yir avian savant
tae ma big generous pal wi the ever open fridge
ma wee pile ae guano oan this hamely windae sill
tae aw ma pals doon the broomielaw an oot tae yoker
ma stash ae goodies doonby if yi kin fin it
captain beaky kens the location
tae lovers ae wit and learning in aw the airts
i leave my scraps ae knowledge aw the unconsidered
trifles ive been snappin up[40] oan my travels
tae a certain wee shady gullerina oan muckle flugga
she kens wha i mean i leave ma macho patter

tae aw the chancers numpties an fearties aroon
this bonnie land i leave an unending supply
ae dumps an splats the true endurin legacy
ae fnc gull tae a receptive warld

wraps it up id say be oan ma wey then
flap aff fae here a gracefu circuit
ower yir roof and awa
intae the wide ocean ae the air
nae tears big man luik yir last oan fnc gull
hes no fur turnin an aye remember
there is guid news yit tae hear[41]
wi mony a joke an smile
afore we gang tae davy jones
by way uv flannan isle

Redomones
and
Eye to the Future

The Broch of Glass [1]

Hildina in the broch of glass
Waits for the southern wind
To bring the ships of the Orkney Jarl
To where she is confined.

By day she stands on the highest wall
Looking beyond the tides,
By night her lantern dimly gleams
Through the tower's glassy sides.

At Yule she huddles her feathery cloak
Fast round her body's chill,
In voar she walks o'er the springing grass
Where the broch's stones meet the hill.

Through simmer dim her white skin glints
More bright than the broch's glass walls,
But the golden hairst brings no remead
To Hildina's anguished calls.

In the morning the sea is still and bare,
Her lover sends no release,
The afternoon brings not the hope
That her loveless years may cease.

In his cave below the bird-filled cliff
The Solan Laird sits tight.
Hildina must come at last to him
One merry-dancing night.

Broch: an ancient tower built for defence near the sea;
Solan: gannet

In Balladia [2]

I

Out of the black nor'east, when all hope had almost gone,
See, says Lady Maisie, waving her empty glass, *a ship.*
Surely, yes it was, back from Norroway. The bold Sir Patrick
Himself, crew dog-tired, vessel storm-battered, wrapped around
With finest silks and golden twine, saved from wrack.
Riding that old Dunfermline road, who to meet him but the eldern
knight.
Welcome back, dear Spens, such feats of seamanship!
I'll sort you, pal, Sir Patrick grits, *can't get rid of me.*
King already hammering the vino, *Great to see you, Pat,*
Have a snifter, slowly subsiding in hiccups,
Hauf seas owre, under the regal table
With the Scots lords at his feet.

II

Things were getting fraught at Ushers Well.
Maids complaining about the briny footprints
On the flagstones and the wringing sheets;
The cook miffed that her special dishes, even
The cullen skink, were being slighted; the three sons
Themselves dripping weed and crabs around, scaring
Bejasus out of dogs and horses; parlour-maid with heebies
Every time the youngest looked at her; cocks struck
Dumb without a cockadoodledoo. The old witch-wife
Beginning to find three idle zombies round the house
Not what she'd bargained for. *Out with you,* she says,
With a suitable curse. And off they have to trudge,
Over the machair, crunch on the shells, heads
Disappearing under the lazy swell, back to their place.
And then, the gathering clouds, a rising wind,
Fashes in the flood, returned, unexorcised, for ever.

III

So when her lover grows to giant size, stamping his foot,
And the ship begins to spin and sink, what else to do
But fire off a maroon into the frosty air, shrug on the yellow
Jacket, secure the strings in front with a bow, and blow
More air into the tube. Shoes off, down the slide.
Then, in the water, switch on the light, blow the whistle
And wait. *For God's sake, woman,* says the lifeboat cox
(Her husband, as it happens), *what are you playing at?*
This is the third time this year. Get a grip.

IV

There she is, five months gone, clutching Tam
While he diverts himself with metamorphosis,
Newt and adder, bear and lion,
Slippery, smooth or hairy, any shape,
You name it, while Janet sweats and spits,
Digging her nails in, squashing, stumbling,
Until, for Pete's sake, a red hot iron bar.
Well, sod this for a game of soldiers,
She thinks, and lets him drop. Off he flies,
Back to Elfland or wherever, and she sighs
With relief, catches the Fairy Queen's eye
And giggles. *No man is worth it, dear,*
Believe me, I know. Call me Maeve.
And off they go, Janet behind astride.
I know a good adoption agency, says Maeve.

V

Back home after seven years who knows where,
Crap shiny suit, green suède shoes, utter naff.
See that Elfin Queen, she was a goer, I can tell you.
No kidding. Melrose Sevens, in the refreshment tent,
Shooting a line — deserts, rivers of blood, strange
Roads, magic apples, bags of nookie, lots more.
Can you believe the man? Sold his car to a guy,
Swore it was in good nick, regularly serviced.
First time on the road in seven years,
All the electrics failed. Don't think he means
To deceive, just convinced he has the tongue of truth,
Like all bad poets.

Returning to Lanark [3]

The War
It is still a war, of course, holy or not;
Mansoul lies yet in jeopardy
and the Metropolis of the World is under siege.
Coming by train to Greater Unthank Central,
glass-roofed and sunny with pigeons,
we keep in our pockets not loch shells and grit,
but hologrammed gay credit cards and mobiles.
Thus can the Institute track us, City Hall keep tabs,
Global-Monboddo input the latest data to our profile.
Out in the hinterlands, the no-fly zone,
the oil and drug cartels, militias, mercenaries
grunt and push around the bomb-fragmented flesh.

The Epic
Received convention is to plunge *'in medias res'*.
Begin with that sudden frantic sense of being a stranger;
this is not a world I recognise, the streets
dingy and pot-holed, put-upon and down-ground people
wearing their diseases under cheap naff clothes,
loud-swearing neds and drunks on buses,
the young betrayed to emptiness in homes and schools.
The oracle should speak to all, recount the Fall,
how when you think that it is sorted,
education, health, a kind of justice quite secured,
in creep again the posh-voiced bronzed Corinthians
to sack and burn the nanny-state,
tossing you as a bonus to the corporate wolves,
old pals, old bullies, same old same old Trojan Horse.

The Great Leviathan
See how land shakes and breaks, the coasts dissolve,
waves sweep in, the mountain slides away,
cities flood, reactors crack, the twisters swirl.
Can we no longer trust this solid earth?
We grew up planted on our Scottish rock,
knowing some things were founded fast.
We did not know that wind and rain,
so fresh upon the face, could bring
the curies to the mountain burn,
the rads to lambs, the becquerels to garden produce.
Above the warming tides of long futurity
the bright-faced culprit lurks in open view,
flaunting his winds, his flares, spots and all,
blessing us daily with his kindly light.

Recording for Eddie [4]

That must have been a time of happiness...
With headphones on, the outer voice is muffled.
Crisp words, hard, sharp on a square of brightness,
I have read you aloud, calm, unruffled,
So often, am I doing you justice
Now, closed in a booth, no eyes to contact?
Knitting of ear, eye, voice – that's how trust is
Engendered. Will once more create impact?
"We'll go with number one." But you will notice,
Listening through your poet's radio mast
Tuned to the finest pitch, if what you wrote is
Lacking its dynamic unsurpassed
Felicity. These thistle days show how remote is
Your wilting even in the hardest blast.

Morganstern [5]

Jump
into the sun, he said. And so we did.
Throughout that spacious star we steered and hid
ourselves in sport among its many ways
and secret spots, that fiery teasing maze
of astral language, light that flared and wrought
out lofty naves of unintimidated thought,
and reservoirs of energetic dreams
to feed imagination's jetting streams.
Till, caught by bubbling light, intensely pinned
in cheerful eloquence of solar wind,
we burst out through the flaming photosphere
and found ourselves on course for swinging near
each planet-child of that prolific source.
The first, a place of such dear kindly force
as gave its green compact communities
a thousand couthy opportunities
to bless their folk, enabled us to know
this wind that carried us was love. And so
to a second world, a realm well starred
with hills, with glens, cloud-crossed, full-watered, hard
to traverse, know, even at times to love
entirely, were it not that, caught above
that thistly land, we saw love's light contain
it in a jewelled sonnet. On again
to further worlds: a multilingual Earth,
its satellites of wisdom, moons of mirth;
a belt of asteroids in tumbling race;
a planet with an outward gaze on space
to speculate beyond convention's bounds,
confront whatever overawes, astounds;
and, last, the great gas giant, passion's fire,
erupting, coming out in fine attire.
All breathless, overcome, we left that sun
to rule its empyrean, turned to run
quick to our lesser system. Looking back
in elegiac mood, we watched a black
advancing shadow of eclipse move slow
across the star's face, full concealment, no
mere transit this, the real deal. Was this
the way to say goodbye, blankly dismiss

all we had known? Yet just at final blink,
before the dark, a bead of light, the chink
of radiance we'd read about, a ring
effect with jewel bursting out, what bling!
We hugged each other, shared such joys.
See, on our screens. The diamond, ah boys,
the diamond!

*(The "diamond ring" effect is a feature of many solar eclipses,
immediately before or after the moment of full eclipse.)*

Maighstir Norman [6]

It is disconcerting, to say the least,
that a man in my position
cannot walk at ease to relish
this highland landscape of his fathers
without a lean Zen Calvinist
dominie striding before,
flicking his fags aside
and jabbing a long sardonic finger
hither and yon to pick out
this and that bird and ben,
frog and loch, stag and burn,
saying, Here is a piece of reality
and see, it is a jewel,
shaped in my language, but not to crystal,
only to its own essential self.

Plato inverted, truth drawn from shadow:
basking shark resurfaced,
   deer skeleton refleshed,
      recodified amazing mister toad.

Day on the Hill [7]

To know that mountain, make an early start
If you want to savour what it has to give.
You'll never take in all, as long's you live.
Yet stride its natural range and know its art –

Each crag a novel, every burn a tale,
Bog-myrtle, bracken, heather, sketching clear
So many small harmonious smile- and tear-
Inducing truths – to temper History's gale

And guide the skeins of wild returning geese.
Do not omit to stoop and study flowers
Or stones, poems that concentrate the powers
Of larger works – for all is of a piece.

Come from the hill at last in evening glow,
Richer through knowledge of a real Munro.

Callanish [8]

With the others, he stands on the skyline,
prim and dignifies, erect in stern propriety,
a Wee Free minister to the life.
By him, a cailleach with her creel
bends in centuries' submissiveness.
The rest, more indistinct, a misty
congregation of anonymous faithful,
make up the circle round their god.
Come closer, see, they are mere stones.
Religion's archetypal image, senseless
and unthinking ring of faith adoring
elevated megalithic vacancy.

Sheep in Harris

Surly old guy
firmly settled on the tarmac verge
not shifting for you
or anybody.

Two young sparks
full of testosterone
ramming horns in rivalry
ignoring swerving cars.

Desolate mother
silent by the carriageway
unable to leave her precious child
lying in blood.

Sheep, eh!

Anger [9]

(i.m. J.T.)

Angers accumulate with passing years,
Some so strong they never go away
But sit in special rooms within the mind
To be avoided, formally revisited,
Or stumbled into on a darkling day.

I do not speak of these, but rather of that
Which follows on the loss of one, not dear to you,
Not marked by tears of your own grief
- Finding the sudden empty desk in front,
Seeing the stunned parents in the mourning pew,

Creating for those left uncomforting respite
Within the classroom's calm routines.
Is it professional anger at a talent's waste,
Frustrated vanity of Dominie Pygmalion
Losing another host for vital cultural genes?

Nothing so cold upon that sunny day
When in the sandstone street of a small Border town
I listened to his friend tell how, the hired car parked,
They went to view the Pentland Firth,
Which hunched its back and coldly licked him down,

Taking from that rock at Durness all his
Seventeen-year-old enthusiasm, quiet smile,
Amused intelligence, a proud new pass
In Higher English, no genius but a dogged wish
To shine somehow, like Sage Carlyle,

Whose birthplace he grew up beside.
I felt that moment's heat of anger soon subside,
Succeeded by this chill occasionally returning tide.

Horatian Ode [10]

(i.m. Joseph P. (Joe) O'Neill, 1929-2008)

The rain drenched a grey Glasgow when we said
Goodbye to you, Joe, in your red church.
Your friends, who knelt or raised the cup and wafer
Or merely sat in grace,

Could not but feel your warming presence rise
To fill the space. Neither eucharist nor
Formula responses, not the singer
Nor the liturgy,

Could match that genial heat that stirred the memory –
The kindly chair of meetings, sudden laughs,
A slight acerbity, humane analysis
Of poets' passion.

Intrigued to hear about a past self, Brother
Francis, to recognise you in "Our Dad"
So praised by grown-up son and daughter,
To share the priest's "My friend".

What sound did that occasion lack for me?
Your voice in "She moved through the fair"
As you so often sang it long ago,
Setting the Irish in you free.

What more was missing? Language at its best –
Some lines of Yeats, perhaps – the tongues of child
And scholar too? I think you would have liked
To hear a word of Gaelic,

And Latin, of course, some Horace, I feel –
Integer vitae scelerisque purus
Non eget Mauris jaculis, neque arcu... .
Nothing to fear, Joe, at the end.

Remembering Jimmy [11]

(i.m. James Inglis)

I didn't tumble to your trick
at first, merely felt disconcerted
looking at your glass eye while
the good one inspected me unnoticed.
That was at my interview, but still
thirty years later I was being caught out.

"Take a minute now to remember Jimmy
as you would wish to remember him,"
your son said at the crem the other day.

Only a minute indeed,
              as the curtains closed.

The slightly bandy walk along the corridor,
the department meeting where yours was the only voice
and sixteen seasoned teachers held their wheesht,
the brisk and sudden rollocking succeeded
by the throaty chuckle and a one-eyed humorous glint.

Intellectual rigour grafted on to humane passion,
the constitutional authoritarian, unsentimental man of feeling,
pugnacious pacifist,
a vegetarian who'd gnaw an argument's wasteful flesh
and spit out bones of logic.
Yon's the true democratic intellect.

I have seen your video
modelling good classroom practice;
"Voltaire imparts Belles Lettres to the Gilded Airdrieonian Youth".
Small wonder your professional memorials are courses
for the unchallenged and the supernormal,
wider horizons for the later learner.....

Other things surprised me.
I did not know the grandpa who knew the names of plants,
the gardener, the concert-goer, art-lover,
brandy connoisseur, the battler for Amnesty International.
But I can believe them.

Every day at ninety-three you took Jenny out
for her breath of air. It took a cauld breath
of snowy Glasgow air to catch you
at the end.

Did Death do a double-take then,
fixing your already dead eye
with his chill gaze, before suddenly
noticing your warm human one
having the last laugh?

Big Guy on the Town ¹²

It is 11:15 in Glasgow a Saturday
the day before St Andrew's Day, yes
you've guessed this is O'Haraspeak, and
it is 2003 and I come off the 44 bus
at Central Station and I go get a Herald Tribune
in W H Smith's on the concourse
because later in the day I will sit with a certain person at home
and do the crossword despite the baseball references
which we do not know but still endure

I walk across to Borders as it starts to rain
and browse among the Scottish books to see if there
is anything new by Eddie Morgan or Donny
and the other boyos but there is nothing
and I pick up Interzone on the way out

I go over to the Woolwich
and the machine doesn't even blink at my PIN
before it sicks out a batch of crumpled Royal Bankies
and I go on up Buchanan Street
across St Vincent Street on the green man
and into the Pier to look at bronzey statuettes

and then right up the steps at the top
into the Royal Concert Hall and wait in line
for tickets to the Children's Christmas Concert
and as I come down the steps again a wee boy
says Who's thon big green guy wi the specs/

and I was standing on the stairs in Dillon's
looking at the middle-aged guy
who looked back at me over his evening paper
with the big guy's photo and the headline
DONALD DEWAR DEAD

Lord of the Dance [13]

(i.m. James Muir)

Sunt lacrimae rerum.........
Virgil got it right, as he did so often,
To make the pious Aeneas weep
Before the images of vanquished Troy.
Yes, tears for things indeed; and all those
Passing outcomes of mortality touch the mind.
So when the music chimes with coffin's
Placement on the final dais, the blessed secular strain
Evoking images of man and wolf
In symbiotic movement on a darkening plain
Upon a silver screen, the tears surprise the eyes,
The mind is touched and we are drawn
Into the celebration of a life.

All lives are exceptional, and each one's life
Sparkles in its own exceptionality.
Thus a youth growing up in Fife and finding love;
A man discovering books and language;
A teacher passing on intangible and priceless wealth;
A husband and father fostering and focusing
A nuclear community of warmth, security and love;
And, too, a writer forming new mortal things
In verse and story – sure, there must be tears,
Brief tears of loss, but more enduring drops
Of happiness that such things have truly lived.

As in the film, where watchers on the plain
See in amazement man and animal create
A new artistic wholeness in their dance,
So we have been blessed in seeing
And being touched by this man's life,
Mortal as all things are, yet shaping in its artistry
An image of enduring things that need no tears.

Thank you, Jim. You tell us yet again,
Whatever life presents, the answer's Yes.
There is no fail, the words and works prevail.
You're right to the end, Jim, write to the end,
Right to the edge, dancing with wolves.

A Hero of the New World [14]

After the dusty parade in the Plaza Mayor   *the main square*
by the League of Youth
and the veterans of the War
of One Hundred Days,

after old Esteban has murdered 'The Flowers of the Forest'
on his faded pipes
and folded them away
for another year,

the doctor and the chief of police
resume their unending chess game
outside the Café Tierras Altas   *the Highlands Café*
over a whisky-soda,

Angus García and Hector Chisolmo
lead their mestizo teams to battle   *mixed race*
with a pigskin ball
in the hour before the dark,

and the wind that blows without obstruction
between the Cordillera and the Southern Ocean   *the Andes mountain range*
divides around the statue
of El Abuelito Escocés   *the Scottish*
Grandad

Libertador of Nueva Alba,   *Liberator*
Friend of the Caudillo,   *the Leader*
exile from his distant North.
In a different age he came,

shepherd in his calling,
scholar in his dreams,
soldier in a new land's extremity,
Gaelic, English, Spanish on his tongue.

With the mountains in his eyes,
the northern seas within his mind,
he stands in his own future, in the unceasing wind
across the horizontal grass.

Between the condor and the albatross
the golden eagle hovers still.

Las Cabras [15]   *(The Goats)*

They have felled the pines
    in the Arroyo de Sueño   *the Gully of Dream*
where the cicadas whirred
    through the midday heat,
and the 'pisos de lujo'   *luxury flats*
    and the 'ropa de diseño'   *designer*
clothes
reign where the goats
    placed their nimble feet.

In those years the Ermita   *hermitage, shrine*
    was alone on its hill
and the Virgen looked out
    down the lonely track.
Yet the faithful come
    with flowers still
past developers' flags
    and the salesmen's shack.

Above the swish
    of incessant sprinkling,
on the next hillside
    to the newest block,
you may just catch
    a melodious tinkling
as the goatherd drives
    his diminishing flock.

And perhaps there is caught
    on a dried-up thorn
a black and white twist
    of nanny-goat's wool,
or a fragment shed
    from the billy-goat's horn,
and the guests may find,
    with shocked eye-poppings,
a warm and steaming
    cluster of droppings
on the pure green grass
    by a blue-tiled pool.

Boatsang [16]

(From "Barcarola" by Pablo Neruda, *Residencia en la tierra*, 1935.)

Oh gin ye wad but touch ma hert,
gin ye wad but pit yir lips tae ma hert,
yir dentie mou, yir teeth,
gin ye wad pit yir toung laek a reid arra
whaur ma bruckle hert is duntan,
gin ye wad blaw owre ma hert, aside the sea, greetan,
it wad dirl wi a kittlie soun, the soun o the wheels on a dwamie train,
laek shiftan watters,
leaves in hairst,
laek bluid,
wi a soun o a drowie lowe birnan the lift,
dramean laek dwams or brainches or blousters
or the mane o a dowie hythe,
gin ye wad blaw on ma hert aside the sea
laek a whitely ghaist
on the rim o the faem
in the set o the win,
laek a lowsened ghaist, on the strand o the sea, greetan.

Laek a naethin hingan on, laek a deid-bell's jowe,
the sea pents the soun o the hert
in smirr an gloaman on a lanely shore:
nicht faas wi nae misdoot
an its wracked an blae-mirk standart
stowes wi a dirdum o siller plenits.

An the hert stounds bitter laek a roaran buckie,
caas; oh sea, oh coronach, oh mizzled dreid
skailed in mishanters an brucken shouders:
the sea wytes wi its stound
its liggan scaddows, its green puppie-flooers.

Four Sonnets of Garcilaso de la Vega ¹⁷

I
Cuando me paro a contemplar mi estado...

When I pause to take stock of my situation,
And look back over the steps that brought me here,
I find, depending on how misguided my journey was,
I could have landed in a lot worse shit;

But when I pay no heed to the road,
I've no idea how I've landed in such a mess;
I know I reach my end, and indeed I've regretted
Seeing my cares dying with me.

I shall have succeeded in devoting myself clumsily
To Someone who'll know how to ruin and finish me
Whenever she wishes and will relish doing it;

So if my own desire can kill me off,
Hers, which isn't really on my side
And has the power, has no option in the matter.

II
En fin, a vuestras manos he venido....

Okay then, here I am at your door,
Ready to face the inevitable.
Whining about it won't do any good,
Not in the book of rules you've written for me.

Looking back, what has this experience amounted to?
Nothing more than a sustained example
Of how the sharpest cuts are given
In the action of surrender.

I see now that pouring out my feelings
On such a dry and bitter tree
Produced only bad fruit and worse luck.

What I feel now is sympathy for you
As you gain no more satisfaction from my obsession.
All you now can have is pleasure from the final kiss-off.

III
La mar en medio y tierras he dejado...

I've left behind the sea and lands in the midst
Of whatever good I timidly possessed;
Going further away every day,
I've passed peoples, customs, languages.

I'm already distrustful of going back;
I think of remedies in my imagination,
And the one that I hope is most certain is that day
When both life and care will end.

What could save me from any harm
Would be seeing you, Lady, or hoping
For the possibility of hoping without losing it.

But already not seeing you stops me from benefiting,
For if it is not death, I find no remedy,
And if it is, I still won't be able to have any.

IV
Un rata se levanta mi esperanza....

My hopes arose for a while.
But, so weary at having arisen
They fall again, reluctantly leaving
Their place free for mistrust to enter.

Who will suffer such bitter change
From good to ill? Oh, weary heart!
Accustomed after fortune to have prosperity,
It now struggles in the poverty of your state.

I myself shall undertake by force of arms
To shatter a mountain, which another might not break,
Set about very thickly with a thousand obstacles.

Not Death nor prison nor any hindrances
Can prevent me from going to see you, as I wish,
Nor any naked spirit nor man of flesh and bone.

Stone Poem [18]

COMHRUITH
Stone, water, people
leave their trace.
Three streams joined,
folk held this place
between the hills
through change and squall.
Work as one,
share it for all.
COMRIE

Legend for Sisyphus Stone [19]

SISYPHUS do you not see that as you strain and push eternally up against my rough and uncomplaining mass you move toward that ultimate condition of being beyond the now and here and when I slip from sweaty failing grasp as was foredoomed and send you sliding stumbling down to try again it is because you are not fit as yet to stand upon the height of death – the necessary end which you are seeking to evade – giving you still assurance you will reach the peak where light and distance open up before you and you see the unexpected future and rest your hands relaxed and gentle on the rainwashed sunwarmed welcoming STONE

Turn of the Season [20]

Trust me, yon sad familiar ice must crack,
A changing climate will take care of that,
The frozen soil, this grey veneer, the flat
Stone-faced indifference to a people's lack
Of zest, of colour, scent, mouth-filling smack
Of triple-decker language, will take heat – and what
Bright creatures then reclaim their habitat,
Marking anew our glen's neglected track.

While you, who look to see by Andrew's croft
A crisp new birch wood springing to the broch,
Blue haze of butterflies and harebells curled
Around the well, a solan's soar and loft
And heart-arresting plunge into the loch,
Stand guarantors of our enlarging world.

Vision [21]

They are to come, the burgh's best days yet,
The empty shops restocked, all streets alive,
Greyfriars to Midsteeple's ringing net
Of song; beyond, street theatre's pulse and drive.

Under the Dock Park trees those warmer nights
Bring out the dancing couples by a deepened Nith,
With laden barges moored beneath the lights.
Accents and colours mingle here, wherewith

A happier age, an easier world at peace,
Embrace this ancient toun, a new Dumfries.

Cockcrow

I heard a cock's crow faint
before six this morning
under the shared breathing in the bed
beyond the lined curtains
and the double-glazing
above the first traffic noise
over the bungalows and semis –

Not a sharp assertion
as in the light-drenched Sabbath air
it used to come across
the perfect hill-reflecting loch
through the blue peat-smoke
ascending straight from Stewarts' chimney
and in the tobacco-tin-wedged open skylight
to the box-bed and a drowsing boy –

Yet it is good to know
that Chanticleer still lives
hailing a new day in bourgeois land
up by the wind farm
and the pyloned moors

Dominus Reconstructus [22]

Here I sit, the amiable alien,
teleported in from elsewhere,
come to 'inspect' Miss S.,
the student, quivering with nerves
and worksheets. I make
mysterious notes, smile at
appropriate points, bend a quizzical gaze
upon undisconcerted boys
and bold-eyed girls.

When the time is right, I rise
and 'circulate' around the
randomly-assembled groups
feigning discussion of a
non-significant question.
The whispers follow me around:
    'He's awfy tall';
        'There's flooers on his shirt';
            'Does he fancy her?'

Yet could these victims of a
post-permissive age but see behind
the rimless glasses and the smiling
eyes, soft suède loafers,
the jacket and the strides,
to glimpse the crumpled suit,
the polished shoes, that long
black gown with rips and chalkdust,
the hard suspicious weight
in either dangling sleeve
of red-edged hymnbook,
coiling leather tawse,
waiting to rear and loose
the whirlwind of a guid
Scots education
on their soft, indulged, unstretched
and unsuspecting noddles.

A Lear of the Suburbs.

"Enter Lear with Cordelia dead in his arms."

I did not choose this part.
I did not audition with the RSC.
I did not learn the words
Nor was I fitted for the kingly robes.

I did not stand before the Court of Britain
And divide my kingdom.
I did not wander the houseless moor
And rage against the gods,
Calling the winds and rain
To bring down havoc on a corrupted world.
I did not rave and weep,
A poor rejected mad old man.

I have lived my life in quiet streets
Doing the world's necessary work,
Thinking I was happy.

Why then has it come to me
At this late hour of life
To bear this unnatural load?

A Good Day for Mr Pepys

-th July, 166-.
In bed, my wife and I had merry talk.
Thence to the office where did write commission
for Captain Kirk to King's new ship "Ambition".
At Whitehall, waiting on his grace of York,
did speak with Mr Evelyn on the scheme
to mingle blood in dogs, and after dined
with several on a sturdy pie, well wined
and aled. There I found the girl did seem
aimable that I kiss her and toucher sa chose.
In the theatre, saw Nelly entertain
the King and beauteous Lady Castlemaine.
Much beer and oysters kept us till we rose
late. Then home to songs and music, prayers said,
my nightly draught was brought. And so to bed.

View from the Gallery Wall [23]

Ah yes, I'm still here after all the years
That time has taken from you. It appears
That I have worn the better. That young man
You were has withered, as has every one
Of those who followed, standing where you are
In shabby coat or crumpled suit, the star
Of your own life, the Man without a Name
Come yet again to the Beautiful Mrs Graham,
To play your part of dumb adoring fan
Like many another weak besotted man.

It is the eyes that I remember best.
Some, like yours, are over-guarded lest
A depth of feeling should be suddenly apprised
By those around one in the throng, disguised
Through years of Scottish caution. I can read
Most other gazes well, feeding my need
To know how people see me, here arrayed,
Posed with a plume, feeling the rich brocade,
Foot poised as if to step out of the frame
Playing the role of haughty wilful dame.
There is a sort of man who'll frankly dote,
Scanning my lips and eyes, bosom and throat,

Seeming to say, "If you were mine, my girl,
You'd know it, that would really be a whirl",
But other men, as drawn to me, yet fear
That which their nature tells them, hide their leer
Under a mask of something close to hating
And move on past, found out, self-deprecating,
Resenting who I am and what I do,
Feeling that I disdain them through and through,
A false surmise. The women are more shrewd
In apprehending that the pure, the lewd,
Are equally inconsequential, as their gaze
Inspects my height and elegance, surveys
The bodice and the skirt, the hat, the hair,
The slightly sullen look of near-despair.
Here, they deduce, the statement of a life,
I the possession, I the trophy wife.

Two pairs of eyes determine my whole being.
The first I remember, Tom the artist's, seeing
My emergence at his brushes' strokes,
Staring into my soul as he invokes
The truth of her, the subject of his art,
The Honourable Mary Graham, née Cathcart,
Fair North British heiress, teenage bride,
Society beauty, Perthshire's toast and pride.
She comes to look, both gratified and shy,
Wearing that dress, and stammering, "Why,
Mr Gainsborough, this is wondrous braw!"
Her large eyes then, and later, looked in awe
Until they grew too large, and then, no more.
Tom (her husband)'s eyes I last recall
Being wet. That was before the sudden fall
Of dark about me. Where I stood and why
Within that dark I do not know. But my
Next light was here within this stately room
And here I must remain, so I presume.
In this room the people come and go
Talking of my friend, Thomas Gainsborough,
Who made me stroke by stroke and dot by dot,
Looking at Mrs Graham, whom I am not.

One thing keeps puzzling as I watch you back —
Where have they gone, why do I ever lack
The comfort of their gaze? They came and smiled
And went, they passed and glanced, and thus beguiled
Me in the boredom of my endless stance,
A silver wallflower waiting for a dance,
Tom and Tom and Mary, unreturning,
And all the others after. Are they spurning
The beautiful Mrs Graham? Do I fail
You in some way? I can never be hail-
Fellow-well-met, and yet I look, I trust,
Approachable. Will you decide you must
Go, too? Your hair is white, is that a sign?
The white-haired always go, traverse my line
Of sight for one last time, and then
Are lost.
              This must not happen. Come again!

Elegy on some Gentlemen of Fortune [24]

You had the best of everything,
You, my brave lads, with the curls and moustache,
The elegant villain's beard
And swords with twirly hilt and flashing blade.

The best sets........... Hollywood palaces with panelled walls
In which to clasp the blonde décolletée princess,
Stone-effect castles with their flagstones
And a spiral staircase perfect for swordplay
And a drawbridge to be let down in the nick of time
For that final splendid charge that saves the day.

The best clothes......... ruffles, lace, the floppy hat,
The leather belts and shiny breastplate,
Elegantly distressed tunic,
Those (definitely masculine) tights, an oiled and hairless chest,
And, ah, the boots, the boots, soft and sexy and supple,
The swaggerer's dream.

The best names......... Rudolf and Captain Blood,
Robin of Locksley, Guy of Gisborne, Black Michael (Prince of Sneers),
Scaramouche, d'Artagnan, Zorro with his Mark,
Rupert of Hentzau, and the Captain from Castile........
And all the names behind the names – Errol, both the Douglases,
Basil (swordsman par excellence), Tyrone, Ronald, Burt,
Still alive in monochrome and Glorious Technicolor
(By arrangement with Natalie Kalmuss).

The best lines........ hacked from a thousand scripts
Some nuggets glint: "Swell, sails, and bear us on";
"One for all and all for one"; "I cannot stand a man
Who fights with furniture"; "Rassendyll, you're the finest
Elphberg of them all". Backed by the studio orchestra,
Cheap sentiments hold their potency across the years.

The best exits....... Not for you the pension and the garden,
Long years' confusion in the geriatric ward,
The grey-faced quietus in the hospice bed.
Rather the sudden shock of hero's rapier thrust,
The rapturous kiss behind THE END, the burst of laughter
At the joker's final prank, the impudent salute —
"Au revoir, play-actor!"—and the slow-motion dive
Into the castle moat. Goodbye, goodbye.

You're better out of it, I feel. What have you to do
With ambiguous anti-heroes, ruthless Bonds,
Obsessed fanatics and dysfunctional cops?
How can boots and rapier avail against the suicide bomb,
The serial killer, shock and awe?

Buckle your swashes tight and still remain
In Ruritania, Sherwood and the Spanish Main.
Perhaps in better days your time will come again.

Hello My Lovely ²⁵

I got back to the office late.
She was already sitting there;
my old armchair glowed as if
it couldn't believe its luck.
The way she'd crossed her legs
reminded the lazy frog in my throat
of its licence to jump.
Her eyes were blue-chip pools of ice-water
that mirrored dancing fires of lust.
"Marlowe," she purred. Her voice cut through me
like a chocolate-malted laser beam.
"How can I persuade you to take this job?"............

I went out on the sidewalk,
my knees doing a jazz number on bass
and drums, and called a cab.
"WalMart on Second," I told the hackie.
Her eyes were dark pools of Bovril
on a marble worktop.
"Marlowe," she husked. Her words licked into my ears
like yoghurt on jello.
"Shall I pull over?"..........

I entered the store, my head blowing
trumpet riffs in a smoky cellar.
"Show me your pastrami," I said
to the dame on shelf-packing.
Her eyes were twin pools of green light
signalling Proceed Without Caution.
"Marlowe," she throated. Her tones reminded me
of honey and ice-cream in a silver scoop.
"I can show you the whole deli."..........

I got back to the apartment late,
my stomach jumping to a jive sextet;
I felt like I was covered in dairy products.
I headed for the shower.
Too late.
Her eyes were deep pools of espresso
in an all-night Starbucks.
"Marlowe," she whispered.........

Croque Monsieur [26]

This song is sung by the writer, Greg Buchanan, in the middle of the first act of the musical, Byres Road Nights, outside the Positano Pizzeria.

Intro.   *It's getting to be that season*
    In the early spring of the year;
    The rose is the symbol, the heart is the reason,
    Love must be nimble and wary of treason,
    And speak out loud and clear.

I looked in the morning paper
When I got out of bed,
And there were the Valentine messages
Across the double spread.
The usual protestations
Of sighing, undying passion,
Anonymous declarations
In a sentimental fashion.

    For Pookums still loves his Cuddles
    And Snookums is mad about Podge,
    While Milkmaid gets into muddles
    Without her Farmer Hodge.
    Frodo is yearning for Sam,
    And Gandalf blows kisses to Prue,
    Miss Bennett has hots for Darcy
    And Bigbum will always be true.

But there were two names that were missing,
Names that I looked for in vain.......
    Names that re-echo with bliss in
    My longing hopeful ears,
    Holding the mem'ry of many a kiss in
    The distance of the years......
Names for the parted lovers
Who may never meet again.

Where are you, my Croque Monsieur?
Do you think about Sunny Side Up,
And the days together, alas too few,
When our love was a brimming cup?

We met in a breakfast bistro
On the Boulevard Saint-Michel.
Your croque-monsieur was overdone
And my eggs were frazzled to hell.
You said, We'll always have Paris,
Striking a movie pose,
But little we thought that our film would end,
Each of us losing a beautiful friend
In a *Casablanca* close.

Bunny is mindful of Froggie,
Miss Whiplash is oiling her thong,
Mister Spock is rocking for Jock
And ironing his sarong.
Abelard from East Kilbride
Still sighs for Heloise,
And what Paolo suggests to Francesca
Would make her go weak at the knees.

I scanned the *Herald* pages
With something akin to despair,
Until at the bottom I suddenly saw it
And could hardly believe it was there.

"A loving thought to Sunny Side Up
From a constant Croque Monsieur —
Can we meet some day
In the old café
And study the lunch menu?"

Hamish is faithful to Plummy,
And Mogs loves Bangers and Stu,
While Sunny Side Up feels warm in his tummy
Just thinking of Croque Monsieur.

"Dear Croque Monsieur,
Your Sunny Side Up
Will always be steadfast, always be true.
The Valentine message is always new,
I.....love......you."

Beltane [27]

An ancient Celtic festival

How did the horned god announce his arrival?
Clannad's breathy notes
served for the hooded man.
Where did the Druid stub his mistletoe?
The standing stones have much
to answer for.
On the night of fire and lust
the ash tree is burnt out.

celebrated at the beginning of May

May Day, May Day.
The people's flag is deepest red.
M'aidez, m'aidez.
The workers' cause is done and dead
upon New Labour's barricades.
Un pueblo unido
No será jamás vencido.

Wash my face with dew, my dear,
for I'm to be queen for a day,
and wake me early, sister fear,
for the wolf is on his way.

usually on the first day of the month (Old Style)

I love "old style",
Palladian rather than Gothic,
'Greek' Thomson, not CRM,
frock coats and Empire décolleté,
riding boots, floppy hats,
bows and cravats.
Give us back our eleven days.
April has ten more days to run
before Beltane lights up our dusk.

**a Scottish quarter day, along with Lammas,
Hallowmas and Candlemas**

A mingy lot, the Scotch,
measuring out their days in quarters.
Give us whole days
in the good old fashion,
twenty-four hours for all
that needs to be done,
drinking and singing,
feasting and houghmagandie,
and a good fire besides.

Bonfires are often lit on the hillsides.

Tonight, all are welcome.
This Beltane,
Lord Pitmirkie will lavishly entertain.
A stirk will be roasted
in the flames
for all to partake.
There will be dancing and the usual
ceremonies.
Through the wicker frame
of his place of surveillance,
Strathclyde's finest
will take note of serious offences,
including
the abuse of regulated substances,
with associated dealing,
public drunkenness,
the unauthorised exchange of fluids,
illegal busking,
the making of excessive noise
after the hour of eleven pm,
and arson
of an aggravated kind.

Once Upon a Time in Orcadia [28]

Of course that was only a beginning,
A new Age of Middle-Earth. After the reign of Sauron
Was ended, and Aragorn the Simpleminded ruled
In Gondor with his feudal nonsense;
After the smug High Kindred took their ships
West over sea, while the hobbits in their Shire
Were steeping their hairy feet in ale and baccy,
There were indeed dark times in Mordor.

The mines were shut, the troops dismissed,
Fresh meat a memory, all light and power cut off,
The arrogant occupying victors hunting down
The Dark Power's agents in their deepest caves.
No orc was safe from insult, violence and death,
Our language mocked, our culture crushed,
Our pride in being Orkish turned to dust
Under an alien Coalition's weight.

Just when it seemed that all was lost,
And orcs must face eternal dark-skinned slavery,
Salvation came in words of fire
Out of the Crack of Doom into the ears
Of Shagrat, chosen vessel of the Lord,
Who wrote the Precious Book of Gollum
The Martyr, final Bearer of the Ring
That in the Darkness binds us.

So in these words we triumph,
Sweeping the Rider from his silvered saddle,
Sealing the Dwarf within his jewelled cavern,
Stifling the Hobbit in his hillside burrow,
Reducing pale Gondor's towers to bloody rubble —
"There is no Lord but Gollum
And Shagrat is His Prophet.
Now is the Holy War of Orcs."

And with the new-found oil of Mordor
What cannot we achieve?

The Communication

I have read your letter,
  overlooking the unconventional
    (not to say startling)
      manner of its delivery,

Slitting open the curiously
  decorated envelope
    and withdrawing the single sheet
      of minutely executed text,

Deciphering the exotic handwriting
  in that distinctly Celtic script,
    despite the aesthetically repellent
      viridian-tinted ink,

Pocketing with an abstracted air
  both that faded photograph
    and the high-denomination banknote
      that are so thoughtfully enclosed,

Absorbing the ambiguously-phrased
  grammatically complex
    structures of its contents, and that
      subtlest whiff of menace,

Pausing to re-read and meditate
  upon the amazing revelation held
    implicitly within the brief yet
      elegant final paragraph,

Followed by the bold and flowing,
  almost indecipherable,
    swirls and curlicues
      of your familiar signature.

Such letters are not answered hastily,
  and so forgive what might appear
    to be an inconsiderate delay
      in my eventual reply,

Yet rest assured that even if these present
    non-committal utterances,
        for all their well-intentioned blandness,
        are not what you desire,

Your real concerns will soon and aptly be resolved,
    though at a time and place
        and in a manner you may find
        most disconcerting.

For now, sincerest salutations and farewell.
    In contacting me in this traditional manner
        you have done the right thing. After all,
        what are friends for?

Losing Face

His friends and family were quite adamant,
His face was sacrosanct, no images
On canvas, print or screen could show him
To the wider world. Only his words,
His deeds, his real significance
Should stand for him in history's
Long judgmental record.

Of course, some damage had been
Already done. The snaps of boyhood,
Graduation photos, wedding album,
Newspaper files on an up-and coming
Businessman, soldier, politician, author –
All had to be culled, suppressed, destroyed.
The daubs and sketches of artistic
Friends, cartoonists' squibs,
TV interviews, election posters,
They too were sent into the flames
Kindled by a zealous following.

At last, however, it was finished.
No record anywhere. None could
Point to this or that to refresh a fading
Memory. And in time the personal
Recollections also went into the fires.

No one now to say, *Yes, he could smile,*
Or, *Women found him attractive,*
Or even, *Under that beard
His chin was slightly weak.*

The myths took over.
Who dare challenge these,
The hagiography, the miracles,
The prophecies,
The lies?

American Cross Code

All across the USA
From Manhattan Island to Frisco Bay,
You'll find two friends on each city corner,
One an encourager, the other a warner,
Helping you cross the busy street,
Keeping control of your itchy feet.

Running White Man tells you to go,
Halting the traffic's urgent flow;
Cab and limo and mean machine
Slide to a halt when his shape is seen.
But watch for the drivers doing a right
In a sneaky move against the light.

Then Red Big Hand steps in to be reckoned
Counting you down with each flashing second;
Even before you're fully across,
He's telling you he's now the boss,
And holds you up with his crimson palm
As if to say, Keep still, stay calm.

New York swings from Side to Side,
Chicago has streets about half a mile wide,
Washington cars are official and proud,
LA and Frisco are way out and loud;
But heed your friends all over the land,
Running White Man and Red Big Hand,
And safely walk through the USA,
Surviving to walk another day.

Class Outline

In the old days
you knew where you were with people.
There were the ones who lived
in the posh streets,
villas and semi-detacheds,
bungalows and town houses,
your sort.
There were those who lived less outwardly,
terraces and tenement flats,
courts and cottages,
respectable to the core,
I suppose.
And then there were the less fortunate,
council estates, caravans,
prefabs, that type of thing.
The addresses gave the game away
most of the time,
the streets, the postal codes,
the house names and numbers.
It was pretty clear
if you had the eyes to see.

But now, good heavens,
who are these e-mail people?
Where do they come from,
how do we know if they're the right sort?
Their addresses merely confuse.
What is a .com person?
Sounds rather lowly station, even humble,
tradesman's entrance and all that.
And .co.uk, what's that all about?
Somebody in trade, rather unseemly
to be waving the patriotic banner.
Then there's .ac.uk, they tell me
it stands for 'academic',
terribly worthy, I've no doubt,
but what a bore.
And as for .net, I give up,
I think they let anyone in,
the odds and sods,
a multitude of plebs.
It's not my kind of world any more.
It's just not my world any more.

On the Wireless

Listen,
you back there,
sitting in your car,
doing the hoovering,
reading the morning paper,
can you hear us,
just below the rock rhythms,
off to the edge of Radio Gaga,
Hardsell Channel, Station Dumbo,
that small voice—simply talking.
No, this is not an interview,
not ads, not the three-minute news,
not a bag of soundbites,
not an ego monologue
or a dialogue of the deaf;
this is your actual rational discourse.
Been a long time, eh?
Real sentences, the full works,
relative pronouns, dependent clauses,
even the odd subjunctive.
That's rhetoric, man, the voice of reason.
Subjects?
Whatever the world
may hold of interest
to the enquiring mind
we can provide.
But, careful, there are those,
we shall not name them,
yet you know who,
are out to get us,
so do not be surprised
if the sound should fade,
the white noise swell to a peak,
the neighbouring channels
encroach and overwhelm
our modest undemanding tones.
You will not find us easily again.
Only by random twiddling,
unguided edging slowly
through the bands intently
probing for that utterly

unique phenomenon, a normal
speaking voice, will we once more
make that longed-for contact
that signifies the truly human
civilised achievement
of one mind meeting many others.

POTUS Moment [29]

That is the pose to fix the icon,
arms out from the sides, supporting weight,
clenched fists on the desktop,
head down, viewed from the rear,
silhouette against the Oval Office window.

Familiar in Life-Magazine black and white,
the burdened democrat (actually an attempt
to relieve back pain).
Again in mono, behind the opening credits,
the anguished liberal (really an ageing actor
earning his bread).

Make it your pose too, just as false.
Super-delusions —free world leader,
winning the war on terror, business Big Brother,
doing God's work. Head of troubled Jove,
Atlantean shoulders, fists of Rocky.
Yet can you sense the pain, pretence
and dumb bewilderment —
How did it come to this?

The Irruption of Topsy

Five Siamese cats, all black, white and grey,
Once lived in a mansion in Grantown-on-Spey;
There was Kirsty and Squeegee and Goober and Mouse,
And Chula, the eldest, was head of the house.
They existed together in absolute bliss,
There was never a spit, there was never a hiss;
They placidly slept, ate and washed side by side,
You never saw any cats more dignified.
But all this exploded in mighty furore
When Topsy the Spider Cat came to the door.
She was small, she was striped, she was utterly twee,
She hadn't a trace of high-class pedigree.
She wormed her way in without shred of excuse
And subjected the inmates to vulgar abuse.
She ate from their dishes and slept on their chairs,
She pee'ed in their boxes and chased them upstairs.
It wasn't too long before each Siamese
Was bewailing the loss of their comfort and ease
They debated on ways to escape the intruder
And Chula proclaimed he would imitate Buddha.
He studied his navel in true Eastern manner
And finally entered the feline Nirvana.
Kirsty went walkabout in a great hurry
And contracted liaisons throughout Nairn and Moray.
The whole sordid business so affected poor Goober
That he hijacked a Boeing and flew it to Cuba.
While the last that was heard of our dear friend, young Squeegee,
He was catching the rats on a slow boat to Fiji.
And Mouse took a fit of acute perturbation,
Which led to his going into deep hibernation.
But the cause, little Topsy, has taken her leave
And the five Siamese cats no longer need grieve.
In fact, as I hear, in a very short while,
They can enter retreat on a croft on Black Isle.

(Written for Jean and Catriona in 1976)

189

What the Ancients Did for Us—The Picts

My goodness, where can one begin? All the wonderful ideas and inventions that this talented people developed and passed down to us. We owe so much to them. In their little corner of the northern world, the Picts were a crucible of creativity. We might go as far as to say that civilisation would look very different without their massive contribution. They were truly among the inventors of the modern world.

Paint, for instance......
The Painted Men, as Tacitus, was it, termed them — those bright-hued warriors across the dripping moor, shaking their iron axes, terrifying to enemies in polychromatic nakedness, tattoos and swirly lines, piercings and danglies. Their artistry astounds. And do we not see them still — the faces all flags and funny cats and dogs, the warpaint makeup; mermaids and daggers on biceps and butterflies on bums; boxers and mudwrestlers, streakers and naturists. Thank you, Picts.

And architecture too.....
What a breakthrough that was! Enough of turf and heather, let's use stone for building. After all, we're loaded with the stuff. And so the first small step for men from brochs on the headlands to castles and cathedrals and erotic gherkins, from inscribed and symbol-dripping standing stones to a billion gravestones and war-memorials and birdcrapped statues. *Calgacus, nos morituri te salutamus!*

The matriarchal society......
What's to say? Mother-in-law jokes, *Hail Mary full of grace*, the other Madonna, Spice Girls, and, of course, our own dear Queen.

A strong navy......
Not a lot of people know that. Rule of the seas from Pentland Firth to Pittenweem, from Orkney to Oronsay (at least until the Norskis happened along). From small acorns do mighty hearts of oak arise — Nelson breaking the French line at Trafalgar, *"There's something the matter with our bloody ships today"*, the Falklands Task Force and the U.S. Sixth Fleet. Pity about the peat-burning submarine, though.

But not your language.........
Enigmatic words and names on mossy stones. P-Celt or Q-Celt, or even proto-Celt? Who knows, who will ever know? This is what you never really did for us—give us your histories at first hand, your songs and laws and novels and users' handbooks for Dark Age microwaves and plasma-screen tellies. Your philosophies and How To Get Rich self-help books. Without a language, a people dies from the earth. We should know.

And the best thing you did for us was not give us your religion.......
More than enough of them from other arrogant and credulous sources. Thank you, thank you, thank you.

The Seer of Achnashellach Contemplates Religion

From The Sayings of Seumas, Chapter II, verses 1—10.

1. A great day shall come; and it shall be a day of warm sun with occasional cloud and a few scattered showers from the west that will refresh every croft and garden;

2. And on that day the holy books shall be returned overdue to the library, and everybody's ticket shall be lost.

3. The voices of Allah and Jehovah and God the Father, Son and Holy Ghost shall echo in ever-diminishing cadence down to an ultimate burp;

4. The knives of mutilation shall be transformed into potato-peelers; the thunderbolt of Jehovah and the sword of the Prophet and the Tridents of Christ's Church Militant shall be reduced to Action Man toys; various clerics and purveyors of pious, ponderous, violent or pawky nothings will form an orderly queue at the local Job Centre;

5. The hejab and the chador and the burqa shall blow away in the wind to amaze and perturb the passing seabirds; the hair of the freed women shall stream through every square and the glow of their faces shall radiate in every street.

6. Every church and cathedral and mosque and synagogue shall become a lodging for the homeless, a cafe for the hungry, a pub for the thirsty, a school for the ignorant, or a care-home for abandoned pets.

7. All beards shall be shaved, all locks shall be given fashionable haircuts, all ritual accessories shall be exchanged for Marks and Spencer vouchers.

8. And all people shall come together and join in the harmonious consumption of bacon rolls, accompanied by a glass or two of a good New World Chardonnay;

9. There shall be selected readings from William Blake, and some rousing choruses of "A man's a man for a' that";

10. And much nonsense shall finally perish from the earth.

Creationists Ahoy!

Here they come again like bugs,
out from under their stones,
just when we thought they'd gone to ground
with the manure and the mouldy bones,

ousted by reason, baffled by science
and incontrovertible fact,
dispatched with their cruel delusions,
dismissed, exploded and sacked.

Yet up they rise from the know-nothing bogs
raising their banners on high,
proclaiming the old-time religion
with the same old pig-headed cry:

"Down with Darwin, down with Science,
this Evolution's absurd!
What ain't in the Bible's a God-damned libel
on Heaven's infallible word.

"Down with Enlightenment, down with Reason,
pack them all off to Hell!
We've got the President, got the Congress,
and we're going to get you as well."

So set up the nonsense academies,
endow a claptrap college,
deprive the kids of their right to the truth,
selling Faith instead of Knowledge.

Pretend you can cancel out the years,
turning the clock right back,
binding women and children in servitude
to the vain old men in black.

We can tell you now it'll never wash,
however you splutter and blether.
Facts are chiels that winna ding
and you can't hold up the weather.

You can fool some people some of the time
and yourselves your whole life through,
but the Universe sings to a different air
and its song has no part for you.

From the Pictish Phrase-book

Beware, your mother-in-law is observing us from the gazebo.

Excuse my importunity but is there a seller of sponges in this village?

Can you direct me to a non-circular hotel?

I appear to have trodden in some ferret-manure.

Thank you, I have enough porridge for the moment.

This is not the same cutlery that I used at breakfast.

Ladies, you are mistaken, this is not your bedchamber.

I think you will find that all the wheels should be of equal size.

Is that your father-in-law at the window of the gun-room?

Excuse me, I have an urgent appointment with the village tattoo-remover.

I should of course love to join in the dance, but my sword is rather blunt.

More from the Pictish Phrase-book

Sir, I feel your wolfhound is becoming overly affectionate.

This is truly a fine necklace, madam. Your husbands clearly took great care of their teeth.

So what is the purpose of these deep holes in the floor?

Did your daughter really mean to eat the Harry Potter book I gave her?

Surely these are not bones down there at the bottom?

Pray tell me why no buses run in alternate months.

Yes, I shall descend this ladder if you insist.

I should prefer my ice-cream without mustard if you don't mind.

Do you really need this ladder elsewhere? I may need it to re-ascend.

Please tell room service I do not require the sheep's liver to be actually removed and cooked in my presence.

I am sorry you feel you must go.

It is, I fear, getting rather dark down here.

Grail Quest

Let's see if I've got this quite right.
You're looking for a drinking cup,
Not just any old cup that might
Be used on days the lads are up

In town for races and some fun,
But one particular which sat
On table for the Galilean
Party that reserved a room at

Passover weeks ago, I can't
Remember clearly why or when,
A bunch of scruff, the type who'll rant
Along the streets, some fishermen,

A shepherd maybe, real rough trade,
Come to the city to make trouble,
Believe me, not at all afraid
Of Roman lawcourts, just a rabble.

That crazy preacher was among
Them, whom the Romans nailed to cross,
Judas, the guy that ended hung,
And Simon, who's become their boss.

Anyway, this cup, you want the one
The preacher used to give the toast,
Whatever, who knows what the man
Was doing? There must be a host

Of differing views, considering who
Were present. I could fetch a cup
And say "This is the one for you",
But I'd be making something up.

The fact is, what with dopey Jonah
Doing the washing-up, last week's
Big wedding—look, I'm not a moaner,
But what do you expect from Greeks? —

The turnover in cups and bowls
Has been horrendous just of late.
My potter's bill alone makes holes
In my accounts, I tell you straight.

My best advice to you comes free.
Pop down the road to Simeon's shop
And order his big specialty,
A *Goblet de Luxe*, with every stop

Pulled out to give it eye-appeal,
Bright paint, big handles, knobbly bits,
The tourists think they've got a deal,
It really dazzles when it sits

In state upon a Roman table.
Even better, if you've what's required,
I know a man supremely able,
Not cheap but everywhere admired,

Whose work in silver's really swish.
He'll do a chalice, fine engraved
With all the symbols that you wish,
Any image that is craved.

And if you like, I'd write a line
'Confirming' it's the kosher item.
I'd add some blurb about the wine,
Our own house red, and not to spite 'em,

I'd fatten out the provenance,
Eye-witness statements, sworn and sealed,
Some affidavits, covenants,
All heavy-duty stuff to wield

In any courtroom. You can make
Some fools believe in anything —
A cup, some bits of cloth, a fake
Effect with lights, a choir to sing

Pretentious words, in Greek maybe,
And bingo! you're away in style,
A myth to gull eternity,
To puzzle scholars and beguile

The superstitious ages still
Unborn. And we shall both come in
To big-time bucks. Trust me it will
Be so, for I am Doctor Spin.

Sorry, Chaps

(A spokesman for the Scottish Landowners has suggested that they might consider apologising to the Scottish people for the Highland Clearances.)

"Being a laird means never knowing how to say sorry."

We're sorry the Clearances happened,
We regret that they ever occurred.
Driving you off to the ends of the earth
Was a faux pas just too, too absurd.

We're sorry the Clearances happened,
It was really just meant as a joke.
One moment your clachans were standing,
The next, they were going up in smoke.

We're sorry the Clearances happened,
We hope you can now understand.
We wanted some wool for a sweater
And it all got a bit out of hand.

We're sorry the Clearances happened,
It's just that we hadn't a sou,
Till the accountants came up with a smashing wheeze
For making things tickety-boo.

We're sorry the Clearances happened,
It's a pity you didn't object.
But you all spoke that weird Teuchter lingo
So your feelings were hard to detect.

We're sorry the Clearances happened
And you had to live down by the sea.
But we're sure you can look on the bright side
And do a good cheap B and B.

We're sorry the Clearances happened
And the emigrant ships sailed away.
But we think it turned out for the best
Seeing the rugger your grandkids can play.

We're sorry the Clearances happened,
But it's all part of Nature's great scheme.
We now to the hills can lift our eyes
Where our deer and our grouse roam supreme.

We're sorry the Clearances happened,
But we don't intend being dispossessed,
Since we after all are conserving the land
And jolly well know what is best.

We're sorry the Clearances happened,
But, like you, we're all patriots stout,
And we'll stand firm upon our green wellies,
Till we sell to some Arab or Kraut.

Monarchs of the Glen

The people of the Highlands, it pains me to say it, do not possess their own land.
It may have been Finlay who left the Beefeater gin bottle in the ha-ha.
Torquil, they tell me, writes occasional letters to the *Daily Telegraph*.
Strictly speaking, there are no lairds in the Highlands.
Kirsty, you might say, drives her Range Rover like a bat out of hell.
Morag, paradoxically, holds holistic healing sessions in the Lodge Cottage.
Every estate has a proprietor (human or corporate).
Shona, I have heard, was Head Girl at Cheltenham Ladies College.
It was probably Fergus who cleaned his Purdeys on the kitchen table.
Caledonia, stern and wild, fit nurse for Melancholy's child.
Fiona, strange to say, has opened a craft boutique beside the Estate Office.
Catriona, we believe, has had a thing with a Cambridge Rugger Blue.
Things are, however, beginning slowly to change.
It was certainly Farquhar who drove home sozzled from the Village Games.
Rory has sometimes toyed with the notion of learning Gaelic.
From scenes like these Auld Scotia's grandeur springs.

Welcome

Welcome to this land.
Welcome to you all —
you plumbers and cleaners,
  doctors and nurses,
    busdrivers and shopkeepers,
      students and language-learners,
chefs and restaurateurs,
  checkout ladies, shelfstackers,
    assemblers and mechanics,
      diggers, shovellers, fruitpickers,
mothers with baby buggies,
  housewives with polybags,
    fathers with mobiles,
      children with wide eyes —
welcome to you whatever your land.

And thank you for coming,
  for your skills and your ideals,
    for your smiles and your optimism,
      for putting up with our insults and assaults,
        for doing the jobs we don't want,
for making our streets more colourful,
  our buses more polyglot,
    our cuisine more interesting,
      our minds more open.

We need you, oh how we need you.
  Keep on coming.

Symposium in the Park with George [30]

(George Elder Davie, died 20/03/07)

Philosophy? — you mean, for everyone?
But we disposed of that years ago in favour of sociology.

Democracy? —yes, we already give all pupils the same curriculum,
though there will always be necessary hierarchies.

Intellect? — we prefer to ensure that all teachers are trained
in the best techniques, so how much they actually know is irrelevant.

A Scottish education? — Ah, there our students are well prepared
for the culture of Scotland – MacJobs and debt management.

*The Democratic Intellect? Still seems like a good idea to me.
Worth trying some day.*

Social Education Period [31]

How do you make a Republican?
Here is how one was formed.

It was to be a great National day
that Coronation June, the Service
in Saint Giles', giving the Scots
a little sense of sharing London's
glitter. Thus the Honours
brought from the Castle Tower,
the peerage and the provosts,
professors and the like, douce
bourgeois Scotland's representatives,
with, tucked in neatly, Scotland's Future,
Head Boys and Girls from the Academies.
"Truly an honour to the school," said
Rector Lodge to me and Moira
in his panelled office with the crests.

There was a slight problem getting in,
persuading a Highland polis
to admit me under the rope,
flashing my gold-edged invite,
the main entrance seemingly reserved
for dignitaries in taxis or in limos,
not for sweating teenager in a
tweedy Burton suit.

But, once inside, surely it was
all worthwhile. Stained glass
and organ voluntaries, the morning suits
and special frocks, the Royal Company
of Archers, Knights of the Thistle,
in swish robes and velvet hats.
The Sword of State borne by a skeletal peer,
the Crown on cushion carried
by a sober-for-that-morning duke,
and other bits and pieces
of some ritual significance.
And then, the Queen
herself, young and newly-crowned,
honouring her faithful Scottish subjects
with her Gracious Presence.

And, yes, it was a nice hat. Every
woman said so. The dress cut
with such taste in the slightly passé
New Look style. And, oh, the handbag,
must have cost a bomb in Bond Street.
Her Majesty was well turned out,
a lovely photo for the Tatler.
Just the right note to strike,
enough to comment on, but not
to let those Scots believe they were
being taken seriously as a nation.

Did I feel a let-down then?
Probably, but memory dwines down
towards self-justifying myth.
Yet I am certain that June day
formed, not just in me, the cast of mind
that, ever since, has had no time
for yonder trite and trivial woman
and her unmeriting ridiculous family.

Republic! Bring it on, say I.
Or else take every Derby winner
with his fine rosette
and well-bred snuffle;
crown him King for the year,
a fitting monarch for the fond
and fawning, Royalty-adoring,
top-hat-doffing,
pearls and twin-set coterie.

Royal Wedding

So here we go again, the Abbey or
Saint Pauls, demure princesses under veils,
those yah-yah princelings togged as if for war,
pretending Scottish roots, a love of Wales.

New tawdry fictions hyped by media guile
to cloak them in a spurious relevance
and push their creaking coach another mile
through history's ironic resonance.

Drag out the awful uncles, horsey aunt,
the leathery step-mum and a weirdo dad,
a dimbo brother, Granny Grim and gaunt
old Grandpa – for a day, forget that sad

elusive, unattainable it seems,
enlightened fair republic of our dreams.

BBC Weather Map [32]

And now the weather.

Here is your weather from the BBC
where you are up top.
Just to be clear, folks,
look at the map, this is your country.
See, we have conveniently shrunk it
to put you in your place,
a little bigger than Wales or that Northern Ireland
(They are really below the level of significance),
but you need a special treatment.

Here is England as we know it,
rather different from the impression
given by STV or the major world atlases.
The South-West and the Home Counties claim
their true important place
in Britain's political reality.

There you are, chaps,
snow in the glens, rain in the Central Belt,
high winds in the east.
Get used to it.
Serves you right.
Enjoy the rest of your evening.

Perfect Image

Strolling this summer evening in the city,
I count my blessings as a man of worth.
My business flourishes, my health is pretty
Good for someone of my age and girth.

My modest wife discreetly walks behind,
In sober blacks, appropriately veiled;
My two sons do what young men are inclined
To do these days; my daughters are curtailed

By dutiful obedience to me
And keep within the home, when not at school.
The doors are locked, and I possess the key.
They know it's for their good that I should rule.

This is a sick society in which
We have to live, and thus we keep apart,
Holding our values. So I may grow rich
And yet maintain my purity of heart.

I have my doubts about what schools here peddle,
Encouraging the young to disbelieve
The truths we stand by. Girls should never meddle
Beyond the basics. That would be to weave

A prickly dress of thorns for all. If taught,
They'd want to choose their lives, come from their shell,
Unlike my wife, who knows her place. She's got
The message, veils conceal her bruises well.

My daughters now are of an age to marry,
And properly prepared by skilful knives.
This summer, single flights back home will carry
Both as cousins' designated wives.

I doubt if they'll complain. Last month I took
The family to see a poor blind aunt
Who lives alone, since long ago she took
The wrong path. Sad to see how acid can't

Be gentle as an instrument of honour.
My faithless sister had a fairer face;
She brought her own doom down upon her.
My brother-in-law may know her resting-place.

All such stern forms of justice I uphold.
Discovering my mother's brief affair,
I told on her before her sin was cold,
And watched her stoning in the public square.

Strolling this summer evening in the sun,
I pride myself on my integrity;
Father, husband, giving place to none,

Perfect
        Image of
                Good—
                        P.I.G.

Muckin Oot the Auld Hame.

Faith, sic a boorach yir in the noo, aa this stuff in yir hoose,
Theres a wheen uv brucks beneath yir feet ah kin see ur uv nae mair use.
Leave it tae wis, the specialists, the boys ae the scaffie squad,
It ull aa gang on the dust-cairt when yis gie the approvin nod.

Whit aboot this fitba junk, yer fur dumpin the lot, ah hope,
Its stunted yir minds fur a hunner year, as bad as smokin dope,
The auld firm programmes, the telly chat, the drivellin sports page pap,
The strips an trophies, the scarves an tee-shirts, the chants an souvenir crap?

Awa wi it, fine, an ah tell yis tae, while oor on the declutterin job,
Oo kin stick this pape and proddy cant deep in the lorrys gob.
The flags ae the ludge, the bowler hats, the flute an fenian bands,
The separate schules, the halie blethers, ahl tak them aa aff yir hands.

Ma goad, heres an unco sicht, whit a load ae trash in yir cellar,
Wee Scottie dugs an tartan doilies an records ae Kenneth McKellar,
Div yis hae nae taste, ah ask yis, sprigs ae white heather indeed,
Auld Sunday Posts an the Daily Record, is this aa yis kin read?

An look, fur peety sake, at yon pile ae bottles an cans.
Ahd say yiv a heap ae problems there, an no jist recyclin wans.
Get rid ae the drams, the pint-an-a-nips, the skoals an the slainte mhaths,
The staggers, the punch-ups, the boakt-up pizzas, the stinkin pee on the waas.

Up in the attic here ah see piled mony a lang-deid notion,
Whirlies ae dust obscurin the licht, perpetual clichés in motion,
Here's tae us wha's like us, oh flower of scotland, we're a' jock tamson's bairns,
Clyde-built, coothie, fur auld lang syne—stanes on crumblin cairns.

Yir a collector ae history buiks, ah note, heres mony a foosty tome,
Union betrayal, Bonnie Prince Chairlie, Geneva's tussle wi Rome.
Puir auld Scotland gubbed again, aw! the romantic blether,
Its anither clearance yir needin noo, alang wi the bracken an heather.

* * * * * * *

There yis ur, its a great wee hoose noo that aa the rubbish has went.
Yiv got space fur improvin and DIY, plus room fur enlightenment.

Cycle Puncture ³⁵

.... The spring, the summer,
The childing autumn, angry winter, change
Their wonted liveries, and the mazed world,
By that increase, now knows not which is which.
And this same progeny of evil comes
From our debate, from our dissension.
(A MIDSUMMER NIGHT'S DREAM, ACT 2, SC.1, LINES 111-116)

So it's come round to spring again.
I marvel it dares show its face
After last year's fiasco, when
The shrunken reservoirs froze over
And April's showers dropped hillsides
On a dozen roads. The flooded city
And the shattered coasts lie far beyond
Our local ken but scar our hearts.

It must have been the summer
That began to set the pattern.
All those forest blazes, not in distant Oz
But down our Highland bens,
Along our Border trails; the too
Unseasonable gales that swept
Whole families away
On Hebridean isles.

And autumn, season of mists,
Transformed to over-brilliant Indian
Summer, did we think it normal
That the colours of the fall
Should be accompanied by gorgeous
Flush of blooms, the scent of lilac,
Mowing of lawns on Halloween?
Fireworks in the perfumed evening air.

Last winter, I remember, Christmas
Was no dream in white, New Year
Smiled in mild benevolence,
And startled roses pushed
Their shoots into the February sun.
March heard a fleeting wintry moan,
A blip of blizzard, sudden melt,
And sunny days returned.

And now, it's spring, the sweet spring.
Where are the snowdrops of yesteryear?
The fluttering, dancing daffs delayed,
No pretty maids all in a ring.
The voice of the turtle ne'er heard in the land,
And young man's fancy nightly spurns
The hots of love.
Cuckoo, jug jug, pu-we, tuwittawoo.

The Sea, The Sea [36]

How can I have failed to see this all these years?
The coming tide by Murdo's burn,
Swirling seaweed at Stromeferry pier,
The St Clair's hissing wake up Bressay Sound,
Baltic bright behind the cruise ship sun-deck,
Slick wet sea-lions on their Frisco Bay pontoons,
The beach at Luskentyre, nothing until America,
Those bright perspectives west across
Atlantic or Pacific blank immensity.

Has it taken seventy years and more
To realise that this is all one,
The same expanse, the same enormous glassful,
Drawn from the tap in Glasgow,
Swigged from the plastic bottle,
Drunk from the hand in hillside springs,
Raised from the ocean's breast,
Swirled in clouds across fragmented lands,
Precipitated finally upon uncaring rock
To give it life, the chances to diversify and thrive,
A verdant glow concealing all the sterile underlay,
The irremediable stone?

All that we have, all that we are,
Is but the faint collateral effect
Of oceanic forces, sea's encroachment
On an alien territory by one means or another,
Currents or tides or weather patterns,
Telling us every day, should we choose to listen,
We are the children of Poseidon,
Bright spawn of Ocean, water babies,
Casual spindrift of the restless waves.

The Who

Who goes there, who goes where,
who goes down to the foot of the stair,
who goes halfers, who goes dutch,
who goes into giggles at the slightest touch,
who goes pop, who goes 'fair cop',
wha gaes aff the heid an ower the top,
who goes croak, who goes for broke,
who goes phut and up in smoke,
who's going grey, who's going astray,
who goes not home at the end of the day,
who's gone to the john, the doo-ron-ron,
away with the fairies, gone, clean gone?

Who comes here, who comes near,
who comes combing their golden hair,
who comes wi a lass, who comes to pass,
who comes up trumps at the top of the class,
who comes out in May, who comes out gay,
who comes out in spots when he kneels to pray,
who comes with a swagger, saying 'Hoots mon',
who cometh in triumph through Babylon,
who's coming to dinner, who's coming to save,
who's coming stalking back from the grave,
who came from space, the Other Place,
who came and went without a trace?

Who knows what, who knows ought,
who knows more than diddley-squat,
who knows best, who knows the rest,
who knows the answers to the final test,
who knows their place, who knows it's a race,
who knows the score and who's still in the chase,
who knows he's bidden, who knows you're kiddin,
who knows just where the bodies are hidden,
who knows a man who knows a man
who knows who to get to carry the can,
who knew all along it would end in tears,
but kept it quiet for a couple of beers?

Who comes, who goes,
we can only suppose,
but there's someone somewhere
who knows, who knows.

Catcall

I am the voice inside your head,
I am the chapter waiting to be read,
I am the secret you don't want spread,
I am the cat in the bag.

I am the rotting cheese in the fridge,
I am the troll beneath the bridge,
I am the smoke-signals high on the ridge,
I am the cat in the bag.

I am the hand that tugs your sleeve,
I am the guest who refuses to leave,
I am the bill you're going to receive,
I am the cat in the bag.

Sooner or later I'm going to appear,
Land in your lap with a snarl and a sneer,
Scratch your hand and spill your beer,
So all the neighbours will say, "Oh dear,
That's the cat out of the bag."

The Numerous Conjunction

The When of Four,
the Where of Seven,
describe the ultimate
How of Eleven.

Yet the If of Eight,
the Unless of Ten,
bring Three's Although
and Six's So
together with Nine
again and again.

Why shuts the door
on One and Five,
meeting with Two
in a low-down dive,
so that Twelve looks tense
beside Whither and Whence.

Watershed

Would you recognise the moment
when it comes, all at once, perhaps
as you are sitting at table, talking
of trivial matters, smiling,
sipping coffee or just quietly
looking at each other's faces?
I do not mean "the moment of truth",
nor yet "the breaking point", far less
"decision time" or "the point of no return".
It is that second when a shift in tone,
a sudden sideways glance, withdrawal
of a hand, a smile when no smile should be,
in a second fractionally longer than a second,
tells you that what you had securely
thought was safe, established, part of your life
that you could count upon, has begun to slip,
may be for a time stilled with conscious effort,
anchored with failing hooks and grapnels,
saved and saved again with desperate hope,
increasing rancour, but, being honest,
is now, this very moment, upon the skids,
headed for the tubes,
effectively over.

Writing

Writing is:
the sex life of stationery;
what writing does;
a strategy employed by paper to achieve world domination;
a conspiracy between the past and the present aimed at controlling the future;
the eye's secret weapon against the ear;
the cinema of the intellect;
the necessary wool for knitting a jumper of meaning;
that which "*maketh an exact man*".

there's aye Scotland
aye daonnan always
I eye mi suil I ee
future future future
ay ay ay ay ay ay
sí sí sí sí sí sí
future futur futuro
yo ojo yo ojo jo ull
always sempre siempre
hay siempre escocia

EYE TO THE FUTURE [1]
(A Poem Sequence)

El pueblo unido no será jamás vencido.
(The people united will never be defeated)

I

Better Thegither [2]

Aye, dearie, listen tae yir auntie,
I'm tellin ye, it's no a day fur gaein oot.
Owre mony rough weans hingin roun
Waitin tae gie ye a batterin.

Stick hame wi us, we'll tak care uv ye,
See ye hiv aw ye need, wee bit pocket-money,
Rin aboot in yir ain wee gairden,
Read Oor Wullie in the Sunday Post.

I'll mak some chips tae yir tea,
Furget thae furrin cairry-oots an cafes.
Hame's best, ye'll fin, stick tae whit ye ken.
Ye're jist no up tae the big bad warld.

Ye see, dearie, Auntie kens whit's best fur ye,
Me an Uncle Davie. Aye, we're better thegither, but.

II

Skipping Chant

Three wee doolies cam tae ma gate,
The first wis a laddie a bit ower blate,
Stanes in his pooches tae gie him some wecht
An keep him frae fleein up oot o sicht.

Three wee tumshies cam tae ma hoose,
The second wis a lassie posh-spoken an douce,
Drew a definitive line in the sand,
But the risin tide left her naewhere tae stand.

Three wee numpties cam tae ma door,
The third wis a wifie aw grumpy an soor,
Total no-no, face like fizz,
Couldnae sell scones tae yir Aunty Liz.

"Better thegither, aw safe an soun,"
Fair keen tae drive auld Scotland doun.

III

The Right Hon. PM Speaks [3]

It's right that folk should have a major say
in how their country's run, and right indeed
that they should know their rights. All people need
a right and proper sense of worth, as may

these little nations to the right of us
(somewhere in Europe, if I'm right in thinking)
show example. Right, but still it's blinking
strange when Jocks kick up a real right fuss

about their rightful freedom, when we see
right well that they were never even slightly
wronged. At Eton I learned history rightly
in that respect. It seems quite right that we

require right-thinking Scots to all vote No.
I'm right, I know I'm right, quite right, you know.

IV

The Sleep of Reason

Another day, more threats and gibes and lies –
you'll be alone, you'll be without a friend,
you'll all be poor, unable to defend
against Fate's ills, foul weather, plagues of flies.

Another day, more gibes and lies and threats –
we'll shut your borders, stop your foreign trade,
destroy your money, see you don't get paid,
and send our heavies to collect your debts.

Another day, more lies and threats and gibes –
you're just a shower of idle drunken Jocks,
you haven't got the sense to change your socks,
you live in slums, flea-ridden clans and tribes.

Another day, a week, a month, a year –
the No-No politics of sour-mouthed fear.

V

Stop the Press

So let us praise the Scottish tabloid Press,
who fear no foe, who write the truth, who take
no bribes, who stand up free and pure, and make
the cause of Scotland theirs to fight. God bless

them aw. Weel, maybes aye, or maybes naw.
There's some wad loodly say they ate the pies,
or sellt their grannies' jerseys, tellt the lies
their London bosses wantit, did hee-haw

for Scotland, showing they'd rather dig the dirt
on Tommy, get wee Alec, write their sneers
at Holyrood, make threats and stir up fears
in blaring headlines, do their best to hurt

the present, twist the past and, worst, obstruct
the future. Time to say to them, Get knotted!

VI

The Question

Like in the poster
when the curious children cluster round,
What did you do in the War, Daddy?
and the haunted face reveals
its shame,

So in the mirror
through all those after-years
you'll catch the face that,
when they brought the Future
in a simple question,
could only answer, No.

VII

(a)

I was brought up to be a proper Scot,
proud to be British, honouring the Queen,
stood for the Anthem, seeing no clash between
an Us and Them. I never questioned what
we learned from press and radio, never prayed
that Scotland could be better through a change.
It shocked me, seeing scoundrels rearrange
the world I knew, and in due time I made

the patriotic choice and voted No
against my country. Yet, what did it gain?
a cross on paper changed things not at all.
the land moves on, but folk I meet, although
polite, display faint flickers of disdain –
I cannot face these mirrors on my wall.

(b)

I was brought up to be a proper Scot,
proud to be British, honouring the Queen,
stood for the Anthem, seeing little clash between
an Us and Them. I only questioned what
they told us when I saw that Scotland played
always as second team. I worked for change,
and cheered to see the system rearrange
to bring a better nation. Thus I made

the only rational choice and voted Yes
for Scotland's soul. We play the cards we drew,
with deeper blue and white the saltires fly,
and unarrestably we all progress,
aware, unlike the timid, we've been true –
I can look anybody in the eye.

VIII

The Inner Hebrides from north to south,
out at the map, a knuckle rap for each
one missed, Miss Wylie's sure-fire way to teach
the shapes and names of Scotland, giving mouth

to words of Gaelic, Norse and Scots, soon charged
with history by Miss MacGregor's tales,
how Bruce and Stewart win, how Wallace fails,
and ballads' mysteries, real life enlarged

to art and carried on to Scotland's songs,
Miss Turnbull leading from piano stool,
the wealth of Burns and Hogg and Nairne. That school,
these teachers – to that distant time belongs

my certainty that I can never go
out to betray their work by voting No.

IX

Interview with H.M.

Ah, Mr Cameron, please take a chair.
Can we dispense with all the usual natter?
I'm charged with telling you how much we care
About your handling of this Scottish matter.

You see, we Royals feel a special pull.
My mother read us Burns to great effect;
Charles practised Gaelic at his northern school;
For Will, the democratic intellect

Was fair the jinkies at St Andrew's Uni.
So, be assured, I wear a Scottish hat,
And though your pompous Old Etonian squads
May sneer at it as merely Brigadoon-y,
The Queen of Scots? Yes, I'd be proud as that,
As were my ancestors, against all odds.

X

Mirror Image [5]

hiv yi bin watchin thon telly series,
oan thi noo, furget thi name,
culd be burger, means society ur sumpn,
its aw aboot this rich wee country
jist across the watter fae uz, hiz its ain
parliment n guvrment like, stauns by itsel,
theres this wumman, real smart, guid looker n aw,
shes thi prime minister, leads her party,
jiggles thi ither politicians aroon, kinna coalition,
goat this policy tae mak things better,
sort oot thi money, guid health, schules,
mak life guid fur evribody, no sae much
rich n puir, gangs aw ower thi warl tae,
europe, africa, america like, sees thi big pickcher,
global problems, ken, really coonts fur sumpn,
maks thi wee country respecktit, no a joke,
no jist a part ae a bigger place,
aw thi people there, see, believe in thirsels,
prood ae their hame, no feert ae onythin,
must be a great bit tae live, yon scotland

- culdnae happn here but, see uz danes,
cannae hack it, niver cam tae much,
pure pish, aye, pish, wir better thegither
wi big brither germany, no tae worry,
jerryll see uz richt.

XI

Ingratitude [6]

When the good Sir James at Teba
Threw the heart of Bruce before him
Into the throng of yet-unborn Spain's enemies
And rode to death, fighting its cause,

He did not think a future Spain
Would selfishly rebuff his nation's claim,
Denying the right already won by him
And that noble heart at Bannockburn.

When a company of Scotland's common men
Joined hearts supporting Spanish freedom,
Meeting the Fascist fire on dusty hillsides,
They did not know a future Spain

Would blank their nation's entry
Into a newer International Brigade,
Making a mockery of La Pasionaria's
Outstretched arms beside the Clyde.

XII

The Human Chain – 11/09/13 [7]

It was still early when we reached the place
red-circled on our map, all seven ticked
as present – parents, grannies, kids – with strict
instructions, national headbands, sheets in case

we didn't know the words – then it was time,
hold hands, spread out across our land, a row
extending north to south, full stretch, all go
to make this Nine-Eleven one to rhyme

and sing about in coming years, the way
we outfaced post-imperial rant and whine
with airs of home and strong unbroken line
to will that Yes on referendum day.

Let this spell take, that eager people see
a time when Catalonia shall be free.

XIII

Aye, Man, Aye [8]

Did ye think it wad aw disappear
When the votes were coontit an stacked?
Ye saved yir No-No majority
An thocht it wis settled as fact.

Wae's me ye're awa up the sheuch!
The future is no as ye thocht.
'Yes' is a word ae infinite force
An winna be hushed fur ocht.

Ye're aff oan a journey ye cannae steer,
An booked aw the wey doun the line.
The singers are up at the front ae the bus
An the driver is cheyngin the sign.

The stag has cam frae the wuid,
The eagle is circlin the rocks,
Jeannie is totally oot ae her bottle
An Jock's no gaein back in the box.

XIV

The Verdict [9]

It's history, boys, provides the truest pleasure
to rational man. The present disappoints
with half-controlled events. Its rancorous measure,
mixing chance and bungled policies, disjoints
what future is imagined. Looking back
in calm detachment is the only way
to see how human life has found its track
through time, stumbling, blind, from day to day,
communities and nations, empires too,
that come to judgement in a patterned weave
and hang in our galactic halls for you
to learn the heights that humans may achieve.
To the defeated, History may say Alas,
but to survivors gives a Merit Pass.

Take, for example, that people who have been
my special study. Students come with me
to pace this cool side avenue and see
each portal opening up a new demesne,
a web of data-banks for each rich phase
of this land's story—First and Second King-
doms, British Interlude, that third brief fling
with monarchy before the golden days,
the settled Scots Republic that endures
into the present Northern Commonwealth.
I find its versatility and health
make it a lasting favourite and ensures
the kind continuing gaze of History
upon the threads of Scotland's tapestry.

Riding to Trapalanda

Poems inspired by the life and character of
Robert Bontine Cunninghame Graham

The Passion of Don Roberto [1]

It is not that I love Argentina more than other lands,
because I know well that this country has a cruel heart;
nor that I can make a lot of money from cattle and horses,
because I know that all profits here flow into rich men's pockets;

Nor that I can ever be one of these oppressed Indians or gauchos,
because for them I am a stranger from a distant planet;
but that when I ride over these plains under the endless sky,
I know that 'paja y cielo' will fill my heart   *(grass and sky)*
until I die.

La Pasión de Don Roberto

No es que ame Argentina más que otras tierras
porque yo sé bien que este país tiene un corazón cruel.
Ni tampoco que pueda ganar mucho dinero de ganado y caballos,
porque yo sé que aquí todas las ganancias se caen en los bolsillos de los ricos.

Ni que yo pueda nunca ser uno de estos indios o gauchos oprimidos,
porque para ellos yo soy un extranjero de un planeta lejano.
Sino que cuando ando a caballo sobre estos llanos abajo del cielo infinito
sé que 'paja y cielo' llenará mi corazón
hasta que muera.

(Spanish version by Alan MacGillivray, amended and corrected by W.R.B. Cunninghame Graham of Gartmore and María Cuerda Astorga.

La Pasión de Don Roberto (2)

No es que quiera yo a Argentina más que a otras tierras,
porque bien sé que este país tiene un corazón cruel;
no es que pueda yo ganar un dineral vendiendo vacas o caballos,
porque sé que acá todas las ganancias van a parar en los bolsillos de lao ricos.

No es que pueda yo ser un indio pisado o un gaucho oprimido,
porque para ellos yo soy un extranjero de planeta remote;
aunque cuando voy a caballo por estas llanuras bajo el cielo infinito,
sí sé que me llanarán el corazón 'paja y cielo, cielo y paja'
hasta que muera.

(Spanish version by John C. McIntyre)

Trapalanda [2]

The greens and greys and blues are shining on
my wall as bright as when the painter (was
it Lavery or Creeps? I have to pause
to think) created that Edenic dawn.
The horses run in their tropillas just
as once they did on the unparcelled range,
unshod and silent round the drowsing strange
lost city of the Indios, where I must
in final days arrive, accompanied
by those I rode with in a youthful passion,
Exaltacion, Raimundo, gaucho-fashion,
before these years of loss, Gartmore, dear Chid.

The picture hangs in space, it never was.
The art that should have been transcends all laws.

Meetin in the Mist [3]

(Di Ildefonso Lopez)   *(I.L. says – 'dicir', 'to say' in Galego)*
Amigos, it's graun tae be back hame in Vigo
haein oor ain Galician crack, no tryin
tae talk posh Castilian laek thae fowks doon sooth.

I fair hid my fill o yon thir last twa years
warkin the boats frae Noruega tae the Cabo,
getting on wi different lingos, but nae galego.   *(the dialect of Galicia in*
Spain)

I tell a lee, there wis yin time I hid the taste o't,
up by in Escocia, ye ken whaur 'tis,
neist Irlanda, wind an rain an mist, laek us.

A year past I wis turnt aff my boat in Leith
an hid tae walk a lang bit owre cross-kintra,
aw the wey tae Glesca, winter comin on an aw.

Ae day's end I fand masel beset by mist an cauld,
nae joke, fair perisht on a dreich laigh moss,
dreipin trees, an empty road, a nicht fur ghaists.

Syne oot the mist there rides a man, true cabaleiro,
braid-brimmed hat, cape an bussie baird, hidalgo
tae the life. I greetit him in whit I thocht inglés.

He smilet and spak me back in Christian español.
We chattit like, me driftin back intae galego,
he unnerstaunin weel eneuch, havin steyed in Vigo

wi his new wife langsyne, alas now deid an gane,
juist laek his family hoose nearby, ainly memories.
He gied me cigarettes afore we pairtit.

As I went on ma wey, on luikin back I saw
him still, heich on his cabalo. And syne I ainly saw
a glow frae his cigarro in the mist, whaur yet he sat

nursin his loss, and seein his ghaists.

King Robert IV [4]

(When asked by a lady if it was true that he was the strongest claimant to the Scottish throne and might one day be King of Scotland, Robert Cunninghame Graham replied, "Yes, I believe that is true. And what a three weeks that would be!")

His brief benevolent despotic reign
Saw startling changes made throughout the land.
Blatant respectability was banned
(Except in Edinburgh); trips to Spain
And South America were added to
The school curriculum; a law was made,
Protecting discreet *demi-mondaine* trade;
All titles were abolished, any who
Maltreated horses were condemned to die,
The poor and sick received their rightful dues.
Such misrule gave offence. It came to pass,
One day he saw a guillotine dragged by
The Art Club window, knew he had to choose,
Lit out on horseback for the seas of grass,

Where, last was heard, an exiled king still moves,
Proud, noiseless, printless, upon unshod hooves.

Esperanzas [5]

(Inchmahome, Lake of Menteith)

I

(September, 1906)
Aye, Laird, draw breath afore the grey day's dool.
We've howked awa aa nicht by lantern glow
Tae mak yir leddy's grave. The morn we'll row
Her ower an lay her doon. In yon dunk mool
Will there be hopes as weel tae tyne an leave
Fur worms? The bairns ye niver had, the hoose
Upby ye lost, the ridin days fitloose
Tae seek lost cities, gowd tae fill yir nieve,

The richts o warking men, Scotland remade,
A horses' haven, an Guid kens whit mair.
Pit them there, these fancies, doon in the clay.
She'll haud them safe. Sakes, Laird! Ye've shairly paid
Yir debt tae youth an hope, an ample share.
See, it's getting licht, could be a braw day.

II

(September, 1936.)
My auld grandfaither tellt me he an you
Dug oot this grave ye're lyin here aside,
Tellt me, whit's mair, you were a man could ride
These Menteith roads an parks the haill day through,
Practised lang syne ower aw thae pampas doun
In Sooth America, forbye in Spain.
It's yir advice on that I culd be haein
The noo, seein that I'm aff this eftirnune.

This Spain, ye ken, the bluidy civil war.
A thinkin fellow cannae jist staun by
While honest workers can dae nocht but dee.
I'm shair yersel wad rise an ride, an daur
The deils. Syne frae the grave I hear ye sigh,
"The deid can open mony a livin ee."

*(Los muertos abren los ojos a los que viven — inscribed on the memorial plaque to
Gabriela Cunninghame Graham above her grave.)*

R.B. Cunninghame Graham at Glen Aray [6]

(On the occasion of the dedication of the Neil Munro Memorial, 28th June, 1935.)

They had to pull the Sheriff up the hill
In Campbell dignity. All others walked;
And being a rangy eighty-three, you stalked
(Missing your horse, no doubt), bow-legged and still

Hidalgo every inch, stylish to kill,
Broad-brimmed, with casual scarf, drooped eyes that mocked
Convention. After local bigwigs talked
In clichés about Neil, did you distil

Impromptu essence of Munro? Who'd know?
No one made notes. Within the year you'd died,
An ocean and a continent away.

All Buenos Ayres watched your funeral show,
A President marked Argentina's pride,
And horses followed Don Roberto's clay.

Boats on the Lake [7]

With you Romance was never far away,
Horses on the pampas, disguises in the desert,
Scuffles in the Square, defiance in the House,
The adventure of being Don Roberto never far from mind.

The journey over water has its own emotive place.
SS. Patagonia started it, off to Montevideo
Back in 1870, sea-sick all the way.
So many other voyages in the later decades.

But, capping them all, the ultimate scene-stealers,
The real Arthurian Tennysonian deal.
Boats on the Lake seeking the holy isle,
Separate artistic echoing moments in time.

The lost wife, Gabriela, exiled from the family tombs,
Carried in open boat across the grey waters,
A Lady of Shalott finding her place of peace
And opening with her death the living eyes.

And, last, your own Arthurian departure,
When, from the port, another open boat set out,
A king's descendant borne to his island rest,
While on the mere the pipers' wailing died away.

So, Don Roberto, your life's often harsh reality
Is tempered by these images of motion –
Boats over water, hooves over grass, stories over facts.
Keep on the go, *viejo amigo*, don't let them pin you down.

Barcos en el Lago

Contigo el romance nunca estuvo muy lejos,
Caballos en las pampas, disfraces en el desierto,
Peleas en la plaza, desafío en la Cámara,
La aventura de ser Don Roberto nunca está lejos de la mente.

El viaje sobre el agua tiene su propio lugar emotivo,
El SS Patagonia lo inició, fuera a Montevideo,
Allá por 1870, mareado todo el trayecto.
Tantos otros viajes en las décadas después.

Pero, para colmo, los robos-focos definitivos,
El auténtico artúrico de Tennyson.
Barcos en El Lago en busca de la isla santa,
Distintos momentos artísticos haciendo ecos en el tiempo.

La esposa perdida, Gabriela, exiliada de las tumbas familiares,
Llevado en un bote abierto através de las aguas grises,
Una dama de Shalott hallando su lugar de paz
Y abriendo con su muerte los ojos vivos.

Y, por último, tu propia partida artúrica,
Cuando, desde el puerto, salió otro bote abierto,
El descendiente de un rey llevado a su isla descansa,
Mientras en el lago los gemidos de los gaiteros se extinguieron.

Así, Don Roberto, la realidad de su vida a menudo dura,
Está atemperado por estas imágenes de movimiento:
Barcos sobre agua, pezuñas sobre hierba, historias sobre hechos.
No dejes nunca de moverte, *old friend*, no permitas nunca que te atrapen.

*(Translation into Spanish by W.R.B. Cunninghame Graham of Gartmore
and María Cuerdo Astorga)*

President Graham Speaks to the Nation [8]

"It is now recognised as a major historical turning-point when, after his successful years as a rancher in Texas and his highly profitable commercial ventures in South America, the multi-millionaire entrepreneur Robert Cunninghame Graham was elected President of the United States as a Democrat. His popular image as an adventurer and pioneer on horseback in the Wild West and on the Argentine Pampas undoubtedly contributed greatly to his electoral success.

The following are extracts from his Inauguration Address."

"My fellow Americans and Americanos,
There are some moments in our mighty nation
When strong decisive acts are needed
To restore and raise our reputation.

For far too long big business interests
Have coldly scorned their workers' plight,
Failing to recognise their unions,
Denying them every economic right.

No social benefits of any kind,
Long hours of toil, low rates of pay,
No job security, no care for health,
All this must change – The Eight-Hour Day,

A social contract, Medicare,
Decent housing, holidays with wage,
Seats on the Board, and proper pensions,
I'll see this fixed at every stage.
- - - - - - - - - - - - -
For women too, there must be change.
In memory of my dear lost Gabriela,
A Senate Bill will order punishment
For every foul-mouthed groping fella.
- - - - - - - - - - - - - -
Some racists in the States here think
That Moslem immigrants present a danger,
But I've been all around the world
And been well-treated as a stranger,

As, for example, in Morocco,
Where Moslems welcome to their table
Whoever comes and ask no questions.
So we should equally be able

243

To take in immigrants without suspicion
And let them live and work beside us,
Forgetting travel bans or inquisitions,
Then no non-Yankees will have cause to chide us.

But here's my big plan for the USA.
For far too long our southern neighbour
Has seen us as oppressive 'gringos',
Stealing their land, exploiting labour,

Shutting them out with dogs and fences.
No more of this. I shall decree
All Mexicans be granted civic rights
To live and work here proud and free,

Especially in those states that Yankees stole,
The states with a sound of El Dorado:
California, Oregón, Montana,
Arizona, Texas, Colorado,

Nevada, Nueva Méjico, Idaho,
Even far to the east, Florida,
Where Cubans too will join our nation.
Once more we'll be an international leader

A great Anglo-Hispanic power,
You've heard it here, Amen, Amen,
God Bless America, Viva Méjico,
Manifest Destiny rides again.

Walking to the Island
And Insular Poems

Walking to the Island is a poetic evocation of boyhood summer holidays in the Wester Ross village of Lochcarron in the years during and just after the Second World War.

Introduction

Lochcarron is a village, district and parish in the North-West Highlands, situated between the peninsula of Applecross and the little town of Kyle of Lochalsh. The village runs along the north-western shore of Loch Carron, a loch running from the sea to the valley of Strathcarron. At the western end of the village is the community of Slumbay which overlooks the waters of the loch and stretches down towards Strome Wood and Stromeferry. Below Slumbay is the small community of Dail a'Chladaich (the Field on the Shore), with thirteen houses, five of which have been built in comparatively recent years. When my brother and I used to spend our summer holidays at our grandparents' house in Dail a'Chladaich between the late 1930s and the middle 50s, there were only eight houses. At the end of the road past these houses, there is a very noticeable little hill on a peninsula approached by a path which is covered by the high spring tides on several days throughout the year. For this reason, although it is not in fact permanently separated from the mainland, it is called Slumbay Island, or simply, to locals, the 'Island'. To my brother and me, our family, and to very many others, both locals and visitors, over generations, it was and remains a place of magic, adventure and imagination, to be explored and re-explored through the whole of a lifetime. Within its small compass there are many natural features which are distinctive and familiar, giving the Island its richness and infinite variety.

What follows is an attempt to recapture memories and experiences of a time long gone. Everybody who knows the locations will have different memories and experiences from different times. These happen to be mine, vivid and precious.

Prologue: Jeantown

There is a faint possibility I suppose that the Lochcarron proprietor (there are no lairds in the Highlands that being a Lowland term) could have been an admirer of the novels of Miss Austen when he was thinking of a good name for his new model fishing village on the north shore of the loch but the likeliest reason for his choice was that his wife or daughter was already Jane so Janetown it was and stayed until somebody with a more Scottish sensibility perhaps a cartographer in Edinburgh rechristened it Jeantown as it duly remained until more recent later twentieth-century times fixed permanently on road signs at either end of the long village street between the north-eastern side past the primary school all the way to the south-western side at the Bank of Scotland which I used to pass every day of my summer holiday in those distant late-forties-early fifties years rattling along on auntie's bicycle over the deteriorating tarmacadam surface going to get the messages listed on an old envelope in my grey flannel trousers pocket from various village shops perhaps up as far as Dunkie MacLean's and in to the Post Office in the 'White House' as it was called where newly-married grandparents lived for a time in the 1890s and where now my cousin Mairi Dula worked behind the counter but certainly making my last stop at Kenny Stewart's for the fresh rolls etc and most importantly for the milk ladled out of a churn by another cousin Jeannie Dula into the two small empty milk pails which I then hung from the handlebars steadying them with my right hand as I set off back out of the village trying to control the rattling pails and prevent spilling with the other messages in the front basket and the saddle-bag behind all being a pretty delicate business with no gears on the bike and a dodgy set of brakes past the West Church (as built by my grandfather) and over the Allt a'Chuirn[1] bridge then past Kenny Post's house and the Seceder[2] church (another grandfather's masterpiece) and on up the Broch Mor brae past Dula's croft to the right on Cnoc Gorm[3] and Minnie MacKenzie's bungalow (good old Grandaddy again) way down on the shore until the last stage came into view an almost hidden opening on the left with small birches grasses and brambles beside the unmade stony track descending steeply to the shore road and the row of eight houses (then) leading to the Island including my Grannie's house but a decision to be made namely is it the daredevil straight down Charlie's Brae here or the longer gentler descent by Seonaid's[4] Brae a couple of hundred yards further on (think of the milk) but be a man and Charlie's Brae it will be down to Dail a'Chladaich and journey's end duty done the rest of the day to enjoy.

Dail a' Chladaich (The Shore Meadow) [5]

Down on the Shore Meadow
along the street by the little bay,
eight houses fronted the northward loch
on the Island way.

Charlie's Brae

Balanced at the top, looking down the steep
long straight, pebbled and rutted, water-worn;
rocks at the foot before the shore; a sharp

right turn of the path; Stewarts' garden gate
to left. Should it be chanced as usual
on Nina's bike? Do the brakes still work

as well as last year? Yet, with full milk
pails, perhaps better to dismount and walk
holding the bike, with messages at front

and back, upright and steady. Down you go, sandals
slipping on the stones, one hand on the bars,
the other on the saddle to keep the cycle straight.

Past the bracken and the brambles and the nettles,
the withered primrose clumps, the seeding grass,
until the slope eases and you stand on level

ground, ready to mount again. A smile and wave
to Mrs Stewart in headscarf and full-length
apron, out in gumboots feeding the hens.

Then off, along the road through Murdo's croft.

Stewarts'

"I'm off over to Charlie's," Granny would say,
taking off her knitted shawl with the big buttons
and putting on her black coat and hat, and boots

over two pairs of black stockings, then away along
the road and over Murdo's Burn, and in to Stewarts'
for a Gaelic blether, tea and fresh scones, and a read

of the cups. Not really Charlie's any more. Old Tearlach[6]
long gone; Kenny's now, he of the General Merchant's shop,
cap on bald head, brown shop-coat, measuring lentils and split peas –

black-suited Elder of the West Church on the Sabbath. Actually
two houses joined with byre and sheds in line, drying-green and hedge
fronting the loch. Steep garden patch behind, beside the brae

reaching the road – ill-omened ground, where in distant years
to come young Charlie's sudden death, working the slope,
would mark the end of Stewarts' as we remembered it, shop and all.

Murdo's

A straight pedal now, hundred yards or so, along to Murdo's Burn
(big pool on the seaward side, occasional minnows to be caught,
water boatmen scurrying over the peat-leached surface),

not much of a croft to see, mostly on a slope,
rocky outcrops here and there, the usual clumps of reeds,
a handful of disconsolate sheep wandering at will.

Fachie the cow grazes within the limits of his cipean,[7]
while grey-muzzled Lachie decides not to get up
and bark. Murdo (or Murchadh) too long gone.

The thatched and earthen-floored sad but-and-ben
is occupied (apart from intrusive hens, two cats
and a favourite sheep) by his seemingly aged widow,

Bean Mhuirachaidh[8](*Anglice* Mrs Murdo), no other name
remembered, grubby, tanned and wrinkled,
two rotting stumps of teeth on show when showering

Gaelic endearments on me as I stop the bike
to say hello. A' laochain,[9] you little hero, is her favourite,
and to seal affection, one time she gave a duck egg

for my tea, fresh from her quacking splashing flock
dabbling the effluent below the outlet pipes
of waste and sewage exposed along the shore

at each low tide. Despite the leary look from Granny
at this biological hazard, I duly ate it all, boiled

rock hard and long over the Primus flame.
Beatons'
Old Mrs Beaton, she's fair a targe, as Granny used to say.
Planted firm-set in men's boots, mobcap and apron
on the beaten-earth front yard beside the garden fence

of Willow Bank, she had an abrupt way with non-laying
hens. I stood once in awe to see a frantic cackler,
clamped under her bare left arm, flapping and shedding

dust and terror, as with hard right hand she drew
and twisted the feathered neck until it dangled
long and limp and silent. Boiled fowl and soup

would dress the Beaton kitchen table this Sabbath.
Job done, she went indoors, appearing shortly
to scatter bowls of mealie feed and call her pecking

flock with Gaelic blandishment. Running they came,
mindless of their vanished sister. Not lost, just gone before.
Look lively, ladies. The cailleach[10] has her eye on you.

Roddy Sly's
Back then it looked really out of place,
straight from a South Coast seaside prom,
white and blue bungalow with a picket fence.

It sat uneasily beside the grey or white rendered
cottages, very modern, when Sly built it,
newest on the block. Never saw Rod much when I was there.

away working, I presume, like so many other younger men.
Peggy Ann, of course, was around, and the girls on holiday.
Not too far in the future then the tragedy,

standing up in the rowing boat, I gather,
when over she went, into the Òb[11] and drowned,
not too far out, but deep enough, alas!

The Big Shed
Two fields beyond Rod's before my journey's end,
part of Beaton's croft, mainly for hay,
except for the patch where stood a shed,

the 'Big Shed', as we knew it, Grand-daddy's workshop.
Here were the coffins made in remoter times,
carpentry for houses, churches, smaller jobs.

By the time I knew it he was gone,
leaving only friendly ghosts—workbench with vices,
basic tools, large axe and chopping block,

peat fibres, sawdust underfoot, stacked logs,
and, of course, the Boat, laid up for years,
only occasional tarrings, briefly relaunched

for a demobbed son-in-law, two grandsons,
who'd fish for cuddies with long rods out the stern,
dragging it down the shore on rollers

from the double doors – doors where once I sat
backward on a wooden chair to rest my little arms,
sighting along the .22 barrel to pot tin-cans

out on the littered foreshore of the Òb,
brass shells spilling on the splintered threshold.
Everyone needs a shed-shaped mental space.

The Pump
Central along the Shore Meadow road
was the Pump,
a communal amenity
before the coming of the taps.

But still a useful thing to have.

Good for swishing over muddy boots
when coming off the croft.

Fine for swilling the earth off
newly-howked Kerrs Pinks and Skerry Blues.

Ideal for rinsing the fresh cuddies
straight from the rods and the loch.

And still an absolute necessity for Mrs Murdo
humphing her two full buckets
back to her unimproved insanitary
earth-floored but-and-ben.

Locarno [12]

So journey's end turn in the side path and round the rear of the house park the bike against the black back shed unhook the milk pails and go in through the porch to the kitchen where Granny is probably making bannocks or scones on the big table taking flour or meal out of the kist with the hinged top lid leaning open a good heat in the Aga and either the flat griddle ready on top or the oven door half open "you're back then a' bhalaich [13] did you see anybody interesting?" "just Kenny the Post up at the Post Office and Mary Barney by the Free Church she had me in and gave me a scone with treacle" "my you're fair a lad for the old ladies" bring in the other messages from the bike and sit at the table and pick up my book perhaps A Princess of Mars [14] again from the big library my grandfather built up spread all over the house a bookcase in every room only a vague memory of himself remember him sitting in his black chair in the kitchen laughing down at me when Nina pushed me through the door from the sitting-room me only two years old him not expecting me yet from the train at Strathcarron surprised and delighted later making me a tent out of sacks over poles in the field behind Locarno near the now empty hen-houses and bee-hives when Jim and his friend Duncan wouldn't let me in their proper white one looking in at me beaming no other memories until we come north in January the first year of the war to see him buried out of his own West Church into the graveyard of the Old Church ruined then as it is now Granny now alone in Locarno for the next decade and a half Locarno a strange non-Highland name for a house not Gaelic nor even pretty English but John MacKenzie was not your average Gael a man of international experience and questing mind and thirst for knowledge taking him to America in his youth and to France (the Zone of the Armies) in middle age so no surprise that he was fired with idealism about the League of Nations in the twenties and saw their conferences as a new hope for the world in which he built churches and houses and did the regular sanitary inspections of unhealthy cottages and but-and-bens trundling about on his motor-bike until gradually disappointed no doubt as the hopeful twenties gave way to the strife-darkened thirties and the second great war of the century which he was spared having to witness what with the death of his airman son a Canadian grandson (also an airman) and a son-in-law (my father) so leaving at this moment the two of us the widowed cailleach and the balachan [15] on his summer holiday together in the kitchen of Locarno the ivy-clad house with the dark-green paint set in the middle of the houses of the shore meadow the most distinguished house of the row I always thought then and still do now so many decades since it was forever lost to us.

Gat's

When did they start doing 'semi-detached' in Highland cottages?
The but-and-ben on its own we know,
but when did they start sticking them together?

Tigh an Eilean, the Island House. I'd never thought
why the name – but of course, as my brother said,
Gat had the grazing there many years ago.
Their sheep and cows kept the Island green and clear.
But Bella on her own left all that far behind,
and now her 'natural' son, John Angus,

burned, discharged and back from the war,
in khaki breeks and braces, teaches me to ride a bike
up and down, running behind me, all the Island road,

Stewarts to Carrachan and back, more and more
assured, till I am fit to carry pails of milk
and brave the perils of a shopping trip.

Another memory. Me and my brother
listening to John Angus' wind-up gramophone
and pre-war Scottish comic songs on records,

songs that we sang together, doing the dishes
in years to come, fraternal harmony personified.
Reverend John Angus MacKenzie (as you became},

with what affection now do I remember you!

Danny's

Walking along the Island road, I meet blind Danny,
out with his stick, tapping ahead on the way
to visit whoever. My sandals make no sound

on the grassy verge. When I touch his big hand,
he jumps. "Cò tha sibh?"[16] I tell him I am Seonaidh Kenaidh's [17]
grandson. "Ailean, a' bhalaich.[18] I'll just stop in and have

a blether with your grandmother." I guide him back
and leave him firmly settled in a wicker armchair
in the porch of Locarno, tea and bannocks on the way.

Mission accomplished. We used to go across to Dannys'
of a wartime evening to hear the news. "This is the BBC Home Sehvice.
Heah is the News, and this is John Snegge reading it."

The wireless had two liquid batteries in these pre-electric days.
After the news from Normandy, we'd go back and check the black-out
before the business of lighting the paraffin lamps.

Ali's
Another semi-detached cottage, joined to Dannys',
always to me rather a mystery, out on a limb at the end
of the line. No Ali (or Alasdair), only a visible widow,

Bean Ali,[19] anonymous in customary black,
last house before the Island, often passed
but never entered. What a surprise

in later years to find a sociable welcoming house,
a daughter both visited and visiting, Nansag,
providing tea and chat for cousin and nieces,

a valuable lesson on how perspectives shift
leaving behind that childhood tunnel observation
in favour of the subtler social landscape of maturity.

An Carraghan (The Carrachan)
It is indeed a smallish pillar, as the name suggests.
Did the pre-Free-Kirk, pre-Kirk, pre-Catholic Carranaich[20]
leave offerings at the base, perform strange rites?

I think I have seen a withered spray or two
below the rock. Enough of such fancies.
Good for climbing, great place for picnics.

Sit on the shore side on the dry smooth stones,
looking across to Port-na-Crioch.[21] But best of all
for football on the springy turf towards the road,

and, yes, for cricket through a long unending
summer evening, faintly bemidged, wicket
against the rock, five-a-side if possible, all ages,

tennis ball and varied bats. Was my father there,
a lost familiar amiable ghost? – in spirit certainly,
I like to hope. Back in the almost dark, when ball and bat

are gone from view, only the megalithic Carrachan
sits in its own dim. "You'll sleep tonight", says Granny
in the lamplight. Some memories are of perfect things.

A boy's Arcadia, Tìr nan Òg,[22] the lost domain.

An t-Eilean Sliombagh (The Island)

My brother Jim as I remember used to fulminate against what could happen to Gaelic place-names when ignorant people tried to make them seem more manageable to Southern eyes and ears one of his favourite examples being Slumbay right here above our grandparents' house in Dail a'Chladaich what stupidity these people had giving a beautiful place like Sliombagh the calm or smooth bay an ugly name like Slumbay to make it sound more English they had no feeling or respect for the language and what were the local people thinking of accepting this insult to their home it was a part of the terrible Gaelic Cringe that affects the Highlands to this day with the native Carranaich thinking their language and culture are second-rate and that incomers and strangers know better than they do how to spell and write the names they and their ancestors grew up with and so on and so on he did go on at some length on these matters but who's to say he was wrong but there we have it the western end of Lochcarron heading down towards Strome (Stromeferry No Ferry as the signs now say) the Slumbay cottages above the Shore Meadow and looking down from the top of Seonaid's Brae you see the Island hunched at the end of the (then) unmade-up road with occasional grass in the middle a green leviathan or perhaps whale shape looking at the slow advance in geological time of Attadale across the narrow sea-loch the Island (Not an Island) sitting in its unrecorded history was it left behind in the latest glacial retreat of sullen bleeding ice which dragged the waters northward in past Applecross and Strome however it came to be now it provides an escape a haven a ready-made arcadia for young imaginations best approached on foot regularly every day of my holiday up from the south usually on your own (your mother or brother following their own pursuits and leaving you to your own devices) approaching the Island as I say and deciding which of the three paths to follow the scrambly path up the steep face or the clockwise path round on the flat under the Frenchman's grave across the meadow and on to the little bay or most probably the anti-clockwise route over the rocks straight to the back and the deeper loch on the right and the view across to the steep cliffs coming down to the narrow track at the water's edge and the single-track railway line (no road as yet constructed) so perhaps you might see the moving plume of smoke signalling the progress of the late morning train towards Kyle no company apart from the Dukes' sheep somewhere doing their bit to keep the Island green and free of too much bracken and bog myrtle and awaiting the moment of the collective decision to raise their heads from the grass stop the chewing and head back off the Island in a straggly flock along Dail a'Chladaich and up to Slumbay the day's work done though perhaps Jimmy and Finlay Duke would come down for them early leading their old white horse (which would without fail make a point of scratching both its sides on the tree outside Locarno leaving a few stiff hairs caught in the bark) and lead them up the hill behind Slumbay to their fenced field and pens leaving you to roam over the rocks or the grassy upland leading to the bare top before making your back home probably having seen an approaching shower coming grey and misty up the loch from Strome and beyond so that with the dropping of the dark the Island is left inhabiting its own semi-insularity under the probably grey indifference of another West Highland summer night.

Island Haiku

Rathad a'Mhachair (The Machair Road)

On the 'island' road
summer sandals stir the stones
going and coming

A few hours each year
spring tides force a sudden stop
— the island is born

An Làrach (The Ruined Croft)

Half-seen rocks in grass
forgotten croft, lost people,
near and yet apart

Did they enjoy brief
tidal dreams of liberty
before expulsion?

An Ceum Cas (The Steep Path)

The in-your face way
bracken bog-myrtle twisty
scramble to the top

Sheep of course made it
kept it clear for ageing ladies
having a giggle

Take the scenic route
an island's for walking round
proving that it is

An Uaigh an Fhrangaich (The Frenchman's Grave)

Ledge up on the right
hazel-shaded bluebell carpet
Was he French? Peut-être

Drowned washed-up sailor
probably papist — not fit
for a Free Kirkyard

Write it as romance
if you'd like another truth
in such a setting

Dail an Eilein (The Island Field)

Sheep would have grazed it
cows fenced in — large pats with flies
keeping a green place

Later clumps of reeds
rushes with dark tufted spikes
but still the sheep-tracks

An Tobar (The Well)

You could well miss it
no longer needed over-run
by water-boatmen

Precarious source
drainage from a mini-ben
too near tidal brine

Rubha a'Chonaisg (Gorse Point)

Crawl along the grass
under yellow flowers and thorns
a stab in the knees

A kind of hideout
special for gulls and terns
speckled shells in the green

An t-Òban Molach (The Shingly Cove)

A smooth rounded rock
sandwiches and thermos flask
cousin aunt and me

Hot sun on pebbles
loch water clear and icy
—West Highland summer

Rubha Creagach (Rocky Point)

Slanting slab of stone
pointing out to Attadale
sunken rocks ahead

High tide on each side
dark depths – dim waving weed
keep to the middle

A' Chùbaid (The Pulpit)

An open-air church
a lichened double lectern
sermons in the sun

Did a real preacher
harangue his flock before the loch
here in Free Kirk mode?

Na Linntean (The Pools)

Between sharp-ridged rocks
crabs limpets anemones
await the next tide

Dabble the water
perturb a mini-cosmos
—you mischievous god

Oisean an Eilein (The Corner of the Island)

Watch the tidal flow
too late, and there is no way
home over the ledge

Take the over route
up the green steps and around
the way the ram leads

An t-Sròn (The Nose)

Here we go brave lads
out along the jutting spur
dare to look sheer down

Like a plank to walk
a diving-board to bounce on
—only rocks beneath

An Uaimh (The Cave)

Islands must have caves
Prince Charlie, Bruce, Rob Roy,
all legends need them

Here well maybe so
bracken hides a narrow door
—only for small guys

Dail nan Creagan Mòra (Field of Boulders)

Fit and young easy
to step or jump these giants
bounce along their tops

Left from the Ice Age
perhaps or calved from a cliff
on the deep steep side

Am Mullach (The Summit)

Time to do it – up
the bare grassy-ridged approach
reach the Island top

Now there's Jeannie's bench
then you stood – took in the view
to Patagonia[23]

Beannachd Leibh (Goodbye, and Blessings on You)

I

On a sunny afternoon the drone swings high
above the bay, its camera looking down,
maintaining its surveillance of Slumbay Island,

an animated Google Map, taking in the bracken
and the gorse, the overgrown bog myrtle,
not a living soul or sheep where once the

little paths criss-crossed. Sitting at my laptop screen,
I have the aerial view the boy I was could
never study. And yet so featureless, so dull,

so changed – it comes as a relief to see it slide
off-screen to be replaced by sparkling water
and the houses by the weedy shore. The web-site

tells me how the Island now is designated – SSSI,
"Site of Special Scientific Interest". Well, maybe so.
I did prefer it as another kind of site –

Special and Sacred to the Imagination.

II

Imagine standing on the Island's top, an older me,
looking down upon the postcard view, the Shore Field,
with its air of full-inhabited expanded

New-Millennium affluence. Well-kept houses
renovated, road new-surfaced, cars in drives,
a village suburb now enjoying its good life share.

I can remember when you looked much less secure,
untended, slightly run-down, the occasional van
bringing the shop to the pensioners and the widows.

Still there was Gaelic heard in every cottage,
each house occupied all year round, with families
spread world-wide, remembering it as 'home'.

Under the prospering façade you may observe
the come-and-go of two-week lets, mobile families

who only see the surface, know no names,

speak in alien accents, feel no kinship ties.
Houses renamed to draw the tourist trade
rather than symbolise a native's dream —

'Locarno' no more.

III
(John MacKenzie)

How can you rouse an interest in a good man's life?
It is not a novel, and he is not the villain of the piece,
nor truly 'hero' either, directed through the turns

and twists of plot. Tensions, hatred, greed and strife,
all the ingredients of hit-list biography
are lacking. Can you find some burst of colour,

a passion that can touch imagination, light
the flame of curiosity about a hint of 'deity'
within the seemingly mundane? What was it

drove this son of Ross-shire crofter off to ply his joiner's trade
on Leeds Art Gallery, cross the Atlantic, write
his journal of a fruitless quest for fortune,

found a village self-improvement club, leave (like Wren)
his monuments in stone, decamp in later middle age
to wear a uniform and serve behind the Front?

Longing to be both minister and writer, he broke
the chains of humble birth, narrow religion, ignorance,
achieved both aims in part, and still,

into a new millennium, works by example
and genetic mystery to inspire succeeding family.
Who do you think you are? I am the 'ogha' [24]
of Seonaidh Kenaidh. Because of him,
I am who I am.

IV
(Flora MacDonald)

Was that really you, the serving-maid from Raigmore House[25],
freed for the evening, running with your pals to town
to stand within the hall door and listen to

The Grand Old Man of politics himself, Mr Gladstone,
speaking to the male electors of Inverness?
You who had no vote nor would have for another

thirty years. Not far indeed from your beginning
out on Crowlin Mor,[26] with the other Clearance victims,
a daughter of 'An Righ', the island's king,

a jokey nickname, somehow suggesting status.
(I have stood in the ruined doorway of his croft,
overgrown with nettles and bracken, and wondered

about your girlhood there.) How can that be squared
with the photo I took of you beshawled in bed,
holding your great-grand-daughter, with eyes

in hollow sockets that had seen the spacemen
break earth's bounds in black and white? You lived through
two half-centuries, and have touched me often

in a third. What I best remember of you
are those years of independent widowhood,
moving with resolution among your neighbours,

indulging a fatherless grandson in a summer idyll,
having a Gaelic crack, and holding, while you could,
fast to your ivied cottage by the stony shore.

V
(Lochcarron)

I drove last winter down the well-marked signed
main street, still almost the only street, watching my speed.
Street-lights all the way, reflected in the loch

to the left, speckling the road in an early frost.
No visible night-life. Drams before the telly
behind closed curtains. Pints and Pinot Grigios

in the Hotel Lounge. Spar shop closed, petrol pump
locked up. No walkers, an occasional furtive cat.
Not auntie's bike tonight; I fumble with the switches

of an unfamiliar hired Fiesta, straight from DMK.
This way I rode so many years ago. No Jeantown sign.
A sharp turn left to Slumbay (since the main road

now goes straight to Kishorn). Up the Broch Mor
(no problem for a car), then on and down
the winding metalled road I never cycled

(Charlie's and Seonaid's Braes so long forgotten,
overgrown). Past what was once our own 'Locarno',
until I pull sharp right into the drive

beside a newer house, built by cousins.
I do not knock or ring, straight in and left
into the sitting-room. There he sits alone,

stick ready to hand, smiling, dram already poured.
"Hullo, bro," I say. "Feasgar math."[27]

VI
Haiku – November-December 2016

Last times come by us
without announcement, as when
saying "Oidche mhath",[28]

you smiled from your chair.
In church I touched your coffin
and felt you smiled.

Insular Poems

Prewar

My prewar was brief
and barely remembered;
for everybody else
it was still postwar,
a bearded king,[1]
jobless and jazz,
the League,
wirelesses with liquid batteries,
frontpage small ads
on newspapers,
dictators
on the prowl.

Afterbirth

A newborn second son
home into a cot
in the Lang Toun,[2]
scented air,
linseed oil
and lino rolls,
steamroller chugging
down the street
arousing infant fears,
below the south horizon
rumble of a new war
over Andalusia.

LMS Inverness-Kyle, 1942.

Somewhere along the line from Dingwall
was the invisible boundary.
To the West, the Prohibited Area,[3]

all the way to the sea-lochs
and the isles. Today it is enforced
by a cheerful chaffing private,

a Green Howard by the cloth badge
on his tunic. Unarmed, of course.
A rifle or two on the narrow platform, no doubt.

No need for that, as he jokes
in a strange Sassenach accent,
and checks the passports, allowing the cailleachs

and the bodachs, and the visiting daughters
with their children to cross their own moors
where now the commandos sweat and curse

on alien slopes, and reach the lochside
crofts and clachans beneath the headlands
where fieldglasses and wireless taps

check and monitor and follow
the passing and assembling convoys
before they sally out into the grey distance

where the wolf-packs watch and wait.

View from the Island

Mist sits low on Bidean a' Cheo [4]
down below the sheep fences
to the first potato patch.
I stand upon the Island
and see the moving smoke
along the lochside track
beside the grey water.
Morning train from Inverness,
letters, parcels, milk, papers,
things in brown sacks,
eager men in demob suits.

Returned Exile

What kind of angry man
stops a teenager
walking to the Island
and empties his grievance?
All his money
blocked in Brazil
by selfish nationalists.
First time I heard the name,
Vargas.[5]

A Distant Guitar

At Granny's kitchen table
with the square-patterned oilcloth,
I sit and read (for the third time?)
a volume from my grandfather's
extensive library —
was it *A Princess of Mars,*
The Thief of Bagdad, whatever;
I like to think,
in the light of later years,
it was *The New Chronicles of Don Q* [6] —
brigands in the sierra,
Civil Guards,
goats with bells in the arroyos,
a hawk-faced hidalgo

Grammar Lesson [7]

At the back
of Pongo Wilson's Spanish class,
"poner: to put".
I write the present tense
in my Academy jotter.
Fourth Year Commercial girls
giggle at "pongo: I put".
Mr W. blinks through thick specs.
Sixth Year, Head Boy,
prefect badge on blazer,
I keep a solemn
superior face

On the Banks of Nith
(A Dumfries Youth, 1937-60)

42 George Street, Dumfries, 1937-41

Clinging to the iron railing, I go down the stone stair.
My little legs take big steps, but a big girl holds my hand
Down to the basement kitchen of our neighbour.

Life on four floors must have been a bind,
But I recall mere fragments. Mother up and down
With housework, Dad out to his new office

Or along as elder to St George's, big brother
Making his pals at the Academy Primary,
Maroon 'Tea-Caddy' blazer, avoiding the High School

Scruff along the other end of George Street.
Yet behind it all, scrap of white paper, umbrella,
Czechoslovakia, "Peace in our time", Poland.

First Day, 1940

Not yet five, part of the Easter intake.
First day at school, along past Moat Brae
(Source of Peter Pan, I've later learned)

And up the steps into the primary playground,
Ruled by Donny Boy with fearsome leather belt,
Grim of reputation, though too old for war.

No infant classroom memories of note.
There was a rocking-horse, which I don't remember
Riding. We copied the alphabet, small and capitals,

In lined books with wooden pens and metal nibs,
Blue-black ink from little wells, scared of blotting,
Forming the rounded letters, up and down strokes,

A discipline forgotten in later years. Likewise forgotten
Many of the faces around me at the tiny desks, except
A couple, still in touch after eight decades, bearing

Like me the strokes and blots of time.

Moffat Road, 1941-43

Whoever named the bungalow had a sense
Of history. Caer Edyn, not Gaelic or English,
But Cymric British, as befitted the South-West.

Now we had lawns, front and back, needing to be mown;
A massive beech tree, leaves to be swept, and mast
To be cracked, white hearts to be crunched and eaten;

A gravel drive that might have held the Morris 8,
Had we still owned it (lost to petrol scarcity),
So Dad now cycled to his nearby office;

A vegetable patch for the war effort; green shed
For bikes and tools; and, in the hall, a wonder,
The telephone with blower and a separate listening piece.

Up in the world, it seemed. Town's edge, a nearby farm,
Good dung for fetching in barrows, Dig for Victory.
A 'bel vedere' whence to observe a distant war.

False security, resting on shaky pillars:
A goodwill rental from a council colleague,
A manageable workload, father's continuing health.

Class Photo, 1943

The war is happening elsewhere, turning the corner,
But here it is early summer, and Primary 1
Are having their class photo taken.

One unknown in knitted jumper and one gym slip
(Edith, sitting with Kirsteen): other girls are sweet
In little dresses, special ribbons in their hair.

The boys a mixed bunch, half in blazers,
Half in jackets or shirt-sleeves (David rather pleb
In zip-up). Academy badge (St Michael's rather

Pompous motto – 'Doctrina Promovet '– at the front.
Rear left, the teacher, Mrs Rae, war widow, neat coiffure;
Beside her, who but smug Master Smooth himself,

Pleased to be the pet beside the teacher,
A sign of favour. Yet with a later cynical
Octogenarian eye do I detect a different

Scenario? Lady teacher setting the group,
Making sure that next to her is placed,
Well-combed and crisp, son of the County

Education Officer, both to be noticed
And commented on in home and council office,
"Is she the teacher?" Not bad, can't do any harm.

If so, it is a wasted effort. Within months,
Smooth young master is a fatherless bairn,
Son of a County Council Home Guard widow,

trying to make ends meet.

*(At that time the first two Primary classes were Infants 1 and 2.
Primary 1 was consequently the equivalent of today's P.3)*

Moffat Road, 1943.

When did it begin to go all pear-shaped?
Photos of Dad at home or in khaki
Uniform begin to show a haggard worn-out face,

Too loose a collar, baggy unfilled tunic, tired eyes.
Death's Big-C triumvirs – Deputy County Clerkship,
Home Guard Exercises, Capstan Full Strength –

Marshalling their legions in an ageing throat.
A time of coming home from school to hear delirium
From a bedroom, seeing spoons of brandy in hot milk

To offer easement, all in vain, before a day
When off a taxi up the gravel drive
Comes Auntie Mary Dingwall from the station.

Only a few days until she knots my tie, despite my
Protests, and says it is my duty as a son
And brother to see my father buried

From the church he served as elder. I sit
Between her and my mother, both in new-bought
Black. Yet many years go past before I learn

For her that was the day she said goodbye, not to
Her last brother, but to her only son of girlhood,
Barely acknowledged, a new-century cupboard

Skeleton. Every family has to have one.
More than another century on, I cannot
Think of her as Granny, try though I might.

Moffat Road, 1943-46

As it had to, the Second World War pounded
To its inevitable conclusion in blood and misery.
In classes, we drew in crayon our lurid pictures

Of 'The Second Front'. Stick men on parachutes,
Searchlights, explosions. Omaha could not have
Been more infernal. Caer Edyn saw its own battle.

Reading my library books in the sitting-room corner,
I eavesdropped on our landlord's badgering of Mother,
Pack up and go, I need the house, the rent must rise.

Only words. A father's lingering reputation prevented
Action. And so we stuck it out. VE Day came,
When, guided by a brother's hand, I scaled the ladder

To Caer Edyn's roof and helped to tie the Union Jack
To grey-harled chimney stack, peace perhaps in our time.
VJ Day also, crowds at the Midsteeple, a new age

Of mushroom cloud and Cold War. The end
Of our cold war arrived, goodbye to bungalow-land,
Postwar austerity dawned, a new home across the Nith.

Nissen Hut

How sleek and graceful is a Nissen Hut!
A semi-tubular arch of corrugated iron,
Two half-moon ends of brick or concrete,

Lights or windows where you will,
Crouched down like a half-buried cocoa tin.
So many war- and post-war incarnations.

A decorated chapel on an Orkney isle,
A camp in Perthshire for imprisoned Nazis,
Later a community of small businesses.

In one such Nissen Hut I have a poem,
Inscribed with chisel on a standing stone.
Which will last longest – poem, stone or hut?

The hut I remember, National Restaurant,
Where Mum and I enjoyed a cheap and cheerful lunch,
One and sixpence worth of rationed nourishment.

In that same hut beside the Library,
Postwar school dinners unsurprising daily,
Mince and tatties, jam and semolina,

Heated up and dished from metal trays
By cheery dinner-ladies. Duty teacher
Saying grace before the clack and clatter.

Staff Sonnets

I
English Teacher (I and II), M.S.

Miss Silvey, three things stick with me till now
from those two years in that dark room below
the stairs. The first was when I told you how
I could not read the board. It was all 'Go'

from then. Seat at the front, an eye test, wired
unflattering specs from our new NHS.
Then, secondly, what was it that inspired
your choice of me to read aloud to class,

and not just once? You must have known how I,
true show-off, relished it. And last, at Strome,
each with our bike exchanged a startled eye,
and smiled, vacation meeting far from home.

So many years have passed. An ancient sang.
Regrets? You never wrote, you never rang.

II
English Teacher, III (W.F.McC.)

Inevitably, 'Corky' to III Latin,
returned from war, now trained to teach not kill.
Still the moustache, but swagger stick and hat in
an unseen kit-bag, and not yet the Bill

I came to know as boss, as colleague, bar
companion in 'The Station', training college
teacher, friend in later life, so far
from where you shared dramatic knowledge

and I became familiar with the 'biz',
on the school stage, with lighting board and spots
and floods, with scripts and make-up, all the fizz
of theatre. No doubt you taught us lots

of English stuff as well. I must confide, all
that I recall, you once called me 'bone idle'.

III
English Teacher, IV-VI (D.C.)

He loved John Milton of all bards the most,
and so he gave to us the fullest measure,
from sonnets all the way to Eden Lost,
blind Samson coming as the final treasure.

When young, I envied those cool rimless glasses.
Aloof yet smiling, 'comme de haut en bas',
exemplifying what a touch of class is,
a connoisseur of wine, plus hypochondria,

he, out of all within my Alma Mater,
most influenced the student I was later –
elitist, literatus, poem-tipsy.

I yet recall that Coronation June,
when, drowsing through a summer afternoon,
we listened as he read "The Scholar Gipsy".

IV
Rector (A.L.) (1)

I know he somewhere kept a mortar-board
among his range of formal caps and hats.
Each day in grey striped pants and morning coat,
starched collar, waistcoat and, believe me, spats,

he kept his standards of a public school
within the halls of Scottish education.
His English mission of a master's rule
over the scholars of a semi-nation?

Strange, for he was just a Scottish heid.
Was he aware, perhaps, of playing a role,
conducting prayers, an officer to lead
his Jocks, black gown a prop to hide the hole

of having 'missed' the War? Maybe we can
believe, beneath it all there lay a nicer man.

V
Classics Master (E.A.S.)

Ungainly on his bike each day to school.
In class, however, classicism exact.
'Amo, amas' to Vergil, every rule
and case and tense and usage neatly stacked.

Another side, of course. That 'Roman' sex;
sidestep your Cicero to find Catullus.
"Move over, boy, your endings need some checks."
The blatant nerve of such a man to pull us.

It must be said, I kept myself well wedged.
No entry there. At last the whistle blew.
Eighty offences proven, more alleged.
Two years inside, then off to pastures new.

Old Time, "Labuntur anni", faintly cries.
I still can see his wife's tormented eyes.

VI
Rector (A.L.) (2)

Well, since we're being classical, suppose
we do apply a tragic gloss and look
for fatal flaws, catharsis and, who knows,
a tragic hero. Aristotle's book

should cover our sad bawdy Border lore.
"What can I do?", I was told he said.
"Am I supposed to lurk outside his door
and catch him 'in flagrante'? As the head,

I have some 'dignitas'." It wouldn't wash.
His life was downhill from then on. Not posh,
just petty. Was it a relief, that mode
of 'tragic' ending, when, in Service fig,
the RAF reunion past, a rig
cut him from wreckage on the Carlisle road.

The Arrival of the World.

Perhaps it was the Italians before the war
Who were the first. The café families, Fuscos
And Piolis, were well-established in my earliest

Memories. I don't know if they were picked upon
In '39 and '40, but there their cafes stood, ice-cream
And ginger. And then it was Norwegians,

Khaki uniforms, fairish and tall, based in a Nithside mill,
Social club, 'Norge Hus', beside the statue of Burns;
King of Norway himself in exile down the road.

Later, the POWs, Italian mainly, coloured target patches
On their basic greens, working on farms. I remember
Some cycling unattended through the quiet summer streets,

Regarded as harmless, sun-tanned and amiable.
Late in the war, there were Germans, grey and grubby,
Shovelling coal in the railway yards, passing remarks

About the Schottische frauleins. When hostilities ended,
A couple used to come up our street in civvies,
No longer enemies, invited to tea and some normality

In an uneasy experiment of peace, before returning to
Their broken homeland. I remember Wolfgang,
Alarming name, but not any kind of Hun we'd read about.

And, yes, of course there were GIs. Not many in our
Backwater town, finding their way around on leave
To look up way-out kinsfolk, before the big D-Day.

Tall and lanky John came to visit Mother, brought
By a bond of shared New-World religion,
Christian Science. In later years, he courted her

By post, fancying his chances with an eligible widow.
No luck, however. For me, the embarrassing result
Was being showered with unwearable American clothes,

Coming in parcels as gift-aid to us European poor.
Mother, a woman of some taste, did not insist
That they be worn. Grey flannel and tweed sufficed.

Most exotic of all, refuges from a civil war,
Not true Spanish, but Catalan, the family
Clarasó, don't ignore that final accent.

Señora and her daughters. Visiting Mother,
Why, I never knew, still a mystery.
Shortly, back to Barcelona and dictatorship.

Yet, for me in retrospect, my first exposure
To an enduring fascination with a land
And culture, part of later life.

Strangers within our Gates

Familiar figures on our Dumfries streets,
Down from the Crichton for the afternoon
As part of its enlightened therapy.

Embarrassments of wealthy families
Sent for a 'rest cure'. Slightly different,
Attracting notice of a kindly sort.

Perjink old gent, dark suit with trouser clips,
Grey cap, white sand-shoes, dapper with his gloves,
Pushing a bike, yet never mounting it.

Flamboyant lady, large in tartan cloak,
Made up to kill, wide-armed expansive sweep,
Admonishing the world with loud posh confidence.

And maybe twice a year, the Misses Duguid
Would arrive from Wallasey to stay with us
("Do good, a fine name, we think it's Scotch.")

Visiting poor brother Willie, "a gentle soul,
Not of this world." Mother baked rock buns, scones,
And we would all have tea. William the Silent

Ate everything in sight. His tea-cup emptied,
He'd hold it high, inspect its inside, signal
For a refill. From time to time, he'd catch

My eye and faintly smile. A knowing twinkle
Might suggest he knew quite well what's what,
And where his scones were buttered best.

"Rednose", 1947-53

Regularly of a week-end evening,
Up our street he'd come, with rolled-up raincoat
On his arm, a fashion we all had then.

He'd join our cricket match across the slope,
Two bats, a tennis-ball, telegraph pole outside
The Bishop's garden as our solid wicket.

Not the best of pitches. Cracking tarmac.
An on-drive uphill, the ball comes trickling back;
A drive to leg and it's a long chase down to stop

The ball from disappearing around the corner
Where the main street traffic waits to gulp it down.
John would chase it, stiff-legged, gangly, awkward,

And chuck it back, off-beam, a lassie's throw.
Like Derek, two years older, in the same class;
With Jim from further up, and Derek's younger

Brothers, add in me, a couple more perhaps,
And we'd have enough to play. For John, I think,
We were the only pals he had, even though

The younger ones would call him 'Rednose', cruelly.
But yet he smiled and never seem to mind.
Later, however, he would make his name

And be a hero for his time. Each day
In school, along the corridor, as classes changed,
He would collect his lines, shillings and florins

Wrapped in paper with the horses' names and race,
The school's own turf accountant, doing the biz.
In the boy's lavvies, morning interval,

He'd do his pay-outs, Honest John. Did any girls,
Or even staff, slip him a bet? I hope so.
The rumour was, he made a mint by our

Mid-century modest reckonings. But why?
Later we learned about his heart condition,
(Was that red nose a symptom?), single mother,

Perhaps compulsion to make good somehow
And prove himself. Whatever. Leaving school,
He found an office job, dead end perhaps.

In Edinburgh, some years further on,
My neighbour Jim came over from the Heriot-
Watt to find me in the Old Quad with my mates

Between lectures. "I hear John Manning's died.
His heart, of course." It was a coldish morning,
Which could explain that moisture in our eyes.

Rood Fair, 1952

At morning prayers, standing before the organ
Screen, at his carved oak table ((which, we had heard,
He wanted to have blessed), the Rector said,

"Mr Tradition, the Head Boy, has reminded me
It is the custom for the school to be
Excused all homework on the Rood Fair Thursday.

So it will be." A murmur through the Hall
And a faint flush of pride. So this is Power,
I daftly thought. The Dock Park was the venue

For the evening's jaunt, the blare and dazzle
Of rides and swings, of shooting galleries,
The shies and roll-a-penny stalls, prizes

And sticky foam and toffee apples, all
The usual fairground fun. Three Hostel girls,
Let out for the evening, joined up with us.

One of them (Did I ever know her name?),
Side-saddle in front of me on a garish
Motorbike, impregnable in navy blue

Mackintosh, made my evening with her laugh.
And that was it. Mr Inhibition
Kicked in in usual style. Goodnight, sweet ladies.

A Daily Walk through History

Every morning as I make my way to school,
I walk past History. Out of Maxwelltown
Over the metal bridge into the Royal Burgh.

Look to the right, young man, where Devorgilla's
Auld Brig stands above the Caul. The Whitesands
Wait upon inevitable inundation.

Far down, beyond my schoolward route, a stone
Set in the paving tells in antique print
Where Kirko fell to Captain Bruce's muskets.

Up Buccleuch Street, Burgh Chambers on the left,
Whence Provost and two aged halberdiers
Emerge occasionally, and then Greyfriars

With Burns, the man himself, grey on his plinth.
A big-eyed stony stare, untrue to life.
Behind, the High Street leads to howff, to house,

To grave. Unseen beneath a licensed grocer's
On the right, the bloody spot where Bruce and pals
Made siccar of the Comyn. Round the church,

I pass the founder of the Savings Banks.
Across the street, the little outfitter's
Run by dramatic sisters, with a brother

Lost to the London theatre and films,
Serious stuff, Old Vic, until at last betrayed
To caricature, broad speech and bulging eyes,

The Ealing Studio Jock in black and white,
Downhill to Dad's Army, forever Corporal Fraser.
Last, my favourite bookshop, over to the gates,

Wrought iron – "Here all hope abandon ye".
Go past the Jannie's house and up the drive.
The bell will ring and the day's work begin.

History lies about us in our infancy,
So we may later lie about it to ourselves.

Foresters' Arms, January, mid-1950s

Standing in the crowded bar with Iain,
Holding a pint of export and a Fowler's
Wee Heavy, I chat to a guy who says,

"You're no' a Doonhamer by the way you speak,"
And I say, "No, we came here before the War,
My father's job", and so I tell what it was,

And where we lived. He gives me a look and says,
"I kent your father, fine man that he was.
One thing sure, boy. You never saw him in a pub."

On the Buses, Summer 1953, 1954

Out of school and into work. Well, at least
A summer job before the autumn term,
Conducting buses for the Western SMT.

The badge was an essential. "PSV
Conductor", large and round, always to be shown.
Fine on a dark uniform, less so on dull

Grey dustcoat. A peaked cap, no less, as well.
No use, however, for a six-footer
Collecting fares along the upper deck.

Left at the platform, along with break-time piece.
An eight-hour shift, early or late, summer
Daylight all the time. Morning workers, evening drunks.

Shocks for the bourgeois youth. Never knew that women
Got as drunk as men, spat and swore as much,
How strong the human smell, plus beer and fags.

Best moments? After the ticket rush, the thrill
Of standing on the bumping double-decker,
Riding the roads, feeling the breeze, swaying

And bouncing, leaving a useful legacy
For later life – never to be sick again
On bus or train, on turbulent boat or plane.

An interlude, of course, before life's real deal,
The academic round, terms and exams,
Caught by the nose and tongue – the scent and taste

Of knowledge, power, more than a job.

Lochar Moss, Summer 1957

Out on the peat bog, sunshine, rain, free at last
Of study, exams, the graduation past.
Theodolite on shoulder, temp surveyor.

Where did that come from? Alec on the doorstep
Asking, would you like a summer outdoor job?
The Peat Board needs you to survey the Moss.

So there we are each morning. Alec, driving
The Land Rover; Douglas (not his name), the boss,
About to be married, half-way through his VD jabs;

Three Forestry Commission guys for heavy lifting,
Davie Kirkwood, John McGowan, and the lad,
Measuring poles, sectioned hollow rods, and me.

Department of Agriculture hit squad,
Have Government scientific instrument,
Will travel, into Dumfriesshire's Matto Grosso.

Start at the already-surveyed centre line.
Set up the tripod, check levels, angles, elevation,
Build up the 100-metre grid with wooden posts.

Everything noted – grid references,
Surface variation, depth of peat – square
By square, the taming of the wilderness.

So technical, and me a literary man.
Good mental exercise, but time to notice
So much else – flowers, birds, a deer or two,

The biting clegs. Avoid the sphagnum pools,
Keep the lenses clear of rain, remove one's shirt
To get the sun, some bookish talk with John,

Surprising fan of Aldous Huxley. Did I know
"Doors of Perception"? Is it possible
To obtain mescalin? Not in Dumfries,

I fear, but what do I know? The hippy age
Is almost here. And too the years of school-rooms,
Career and family, being at last a grown-up.

These memories abide, last irresponsible
Weeks. The times, they are a-changing. But
There is an unexpected legacy.

Six decades on, the summer tan long faded
From the torso, I wear in rich abundance
The solar stigmata printed on my skin.

Rosemount Street, 1960

It had at last come to this. The removal
(In two parts) finally done, mother off
To Edinburgh, our third and final home

In Dumfries empty, swept and echoing hollow.
Nothing to do but drive away to Annan flat.
Leave it behind - the childhood years of war,

Austerity, school and varsity, commuting
Down each day to teach - and most, of course,
Loss of father, brother off to Africa,

Mother worn down, glad to be retired, leaving
The memories, the worry, grinding duty.
I close the front door, feel for the Morris key.

But, no, it is not over. Next doors come out.
"You must come in. You'll not have eaten
Anything." And so, the parting meal, the glass

Of homebrew, followed by a second. Time to go
When elbow bumps off the chair arm, and I
Realise I have to drive some lonely miles

In growing dark, with no police, I hope.
And so it ends. Northwards career and
Married life remove me from the friendly toun

Queen of the South, set in your vale of Nith,
"Where Burns lived, toiled and sang", sandstone
Walls, green fields. Why did I not return,

Save fleetingly. So many whom I know
Have never left. Was I mere bird of passage?
Do these verses serve as a belated apologia?

Sonnets to Hugh Macdiarmid,
and Other Scots Poems

Sonnets to Hugh MacDiarmid

I

Hughie, thou shouldst be leevin at this oor
Fur Scotlan culd be daein wi yir crack.
Sin ye depairtit, things are fair aback.
Nae modern pundit speaks wi hauf yir pooer.
Aw scrievers, pressmen, bardies cringe and cooer.
Political correctness gars thaim tak
A fearfu tent o aw they write, an mak
Obeisance tae the mim-mooed goad o soor
Politeness. Naebody maun be offended
By ocht that's said. Treat aw things wi respect.
Pit steeks upo yir tung, let hochs be bended.
Ma Goad, I hear yi gurl. "I'll no be sneckt.,
Gaun gies ma pen, the truth maun be defended.
Nae gude or greatness growes frae bein correct."

*(scrievers: writers. tent: heed. steeks: gags. hochs: hind legs.
gurl: growl. sneckt: shut up.)*

II

I doot if Europe figured gretly in yir thocht
The wey we see it noo. Fur aw yir days
It wis juist empires deein, leavin nocht
But creeds, dictators, wars, a bluidy maze
O hate an fear, that wad hae seemit waur
Nor England's domination owre oor kin.
A peacefu Europe nae yin then micht daur
Tae dream aboot, faur less tae leeve within.
But yit we ken it, an wad hae it last,
Wi Scotlan aye a pairt o't. But we see
It runcht awa, oor future stawn an cast
Upo a midden, Englan's vanity.
"We'll mike ould England grite again", they skreich,
Slitterin aw the land wi racist keech.

*(waur: worse. runcht: wrenched. stawn: stolen. midden: dunghill.
skreich: screech. slitterin: smearing. keech: excrement.)*

III

A damfule English Brexit's whit we'll get,
If ye'll forgie the pun. Yi ken yirsel
Hoo Suddron politicians ayeweys set
Their nation first, an see the lave tae hell.
Whitever ither fowks in ony place
May think or vote, their answer's aye the same,
Pish aff, you sods. "We ah the mahster rice",
An Jocks an Micks an Taffs maun play oor game."
An sae it is wi Brexit. We can vote agin it
Aw we like, it maks nae odds tae Boris,
A Tory nyaff, whitever wey yi spin it,
Wi nae guidwillie mensefu thochties fur us.
Dae thae guys no see that whit they're daen
Is makin dear auld England wee agane?

*(Suddron: Southern. ayeweys: always. lave: rest.
nyaff: worthless conceited person. guidwillie: generous.
mensefu: polite.)*

IV

Weel heh therr, Shewie, hoos it gaun, OK?
Zis no a bummer, aw this lockdoun shite,
Juist stuck in wir hooses, day eftir day,
Nicht eftir nicht, me an the wife gaen gyte.
Still, in a guid cause, keepin wis safe an soun.
No lyk whit yi saw then, lang syne. Nae lees,
Yon Spanish flu killt millions aw around,
Mair nor the War, fowk drappin doun lyk fleas.
An whit did governments dae then? Hee-haw.
Juist heidless chookies every yin, nae clues.
Quite different the day. We've Paw and Maw
Boris an Nicola seein we dinna lose,
Daein the business, kennin when and why
Tae pit the brakes oan hard. Weel, maybe's aye.

(gyte: mad. chookies: chickens.)

V

Ane doolie sessoun cumis tae ilk manis lyf,
Quhidder wi weir or pestilens or wadder,
An sa it wes quhan I in tym o stryf
Socht be aw meanis my dowie spreitis to gadder.
Syn wi a drink in haund I wailt thy buik
Anent the thrissil an the drouthie chiel,
An sic a makaris lift fra it I tuik
I fell into a dwam, an in a reel
I cleckit on anither michtie wark,
In quhilk the Scottis thrissil maun be sene
A bonnie flour amiddis the warldis gret park,
Lufit an respeckit wi clere and sober een.
See weel, my Hugh, an ither bardis fra hence,
Wryte sic a sang for Scotlandis richtfu mense.

(Scripsit Robert Henrysoun)

(doolie: doleful. sessoun: season. weir: war. dowie: sad. wailt: chose.
anent: concerning. drouthie: drunken. lift: encouragement.
dwam: daydream. cleckit: imagined. quhilk: which. mense: honour.)
(Scripsit Robert Henrysoun: the sonnet is modelled on the first lines
of Henryson's 'Testament of Cresseid')

VI

It seems that maist o us, it's fair a thocht,
Sprang frae asylum-seikers i the past,
Forbye the Picts, perhaps, but wha kens ocht
O thaim? Gaels, Norskis, Paddies, evri last
Wee guy, were bustin guts tae lea'e ahint
Their neeboors, wives or rent-man, evri bugger
Wha hid it in fur thaim. If they were skint
Or fleein the polis, psychopath or mugger,
They did a runner, aff tae pastures new.
Sae Bonnie Scotlan jinked intae oor ken.
Aye, aye, I jest, but tak a kindly view
O thae puir chiels wha wash up in oor glen
Or street. They didna chuse their situation.
Perhaps it's time tae be a Rainbow Nation.

VII

Shair, Nort America is brawlie rich
Wi sterry een an fou wi rowstie blethers.
Whill Sooth America shaws aff its feathers,
Its gaupin stangs dreep bluid intil the ditch.
Gret Asia is hame tae hauf the human race
An sune will be the maister o the earth.
Yit naethin's new tae Africa but dearth
An drouth. It ayeweys sits in hinmaist place.
The isles of Oceania dot the sunbricht sea
Illusionary foostie Paradise.
Whill cauld Antarctica neath hettin skies
Prepares tae droun the haill clanjamfrie.
But Europe's still oor ain auld bonnie dame,
Aye tae be lued, an aye tae be oor hame.

(shair: indeed. brawlie: finely. rowstie: blustering.
stangs: wounds. drouth: drought. ayeweys: always.
foostie: musty. clanfamfrie: disorderly crowd.)

(The sonnet is modelled on MacDiarmid's lyric,
'The Bonnie Broukit Bairn'.)

VIII

Losh, Shug, dae yi no think it maun hae been
A stammygaster tae the Laird o Home
Tae fin yi staunin neist him on the scene
O an election? Did the Tories fume
Whan a wee leftie Lallans bardie daured
Tae staun fur Parliament agin the odds?
Aye, aye, yi lost. But still yi shawed the sword.
Nae doot they laucht, laek sleekit sneistie tods.
Weel, they're no lauchin noo. The flude's gane oot.
They're quat upo a steenie tanglit strand,
Wi nae wey back tae gaither ony foot,
Nae ploy, nae wuts, a shilpit donnert band.
Ill-gabbit lees, noo wappens o the Tory
Tae fecht their faes. But yon's anither story.

(stammygaster: unpleasant surprise. sneistie: arrogant.
tods: foxes. quat: forsaken. shilpit: puny. donnert: stupefied.
ill-gabbit: abusive.)

IX

I've jist doonloadit aff the Internet
A photie shawin twa Scot Nats in cahoots,
Yirsel an Don Roberto, luikin set
Tae brenn the hedder in yir guid derk suits,
Douce warriors o a naitional revolution.
Syne jist a baur, but noo the SNP
Fair rewl the reest, daein aw the wark o pushin
Fur Scotlan's independence. We maun see
Hoo muckle stamack aw thae snod perjink
Wee craturs gaither fur the hinmaist fecht
Whan deeds no wirds are needit. Daur we think
They hae the mojo? Yon wad be a sicht,
Oor ain Scottis politicians gettin teuch.
Richt, c'moan pals, we've waited lang eneuch.

(brenn: burn. syne: then. baur: joke. reest: roost.
snod: neat. perjink: prim. hinmaist: ultimate.)

X

I doot if Langholm iver gave a toss,
Whan yi were young, aboot an Auld Firm game,
Whether the Hoops and Gers hid win or loss.
The maist o Scotlan ken it's Scotlan's shame
That fitba focuses sic laithsome hate
Tae poor frae auld releegious clishmaclavers
An keech aw owre oor bonnie kindlie state.
It staps baith men an weans wi ugsome slavers.
Wad we were rid o baith thae donnert teams,
Thur names an strips an chants an glaikit fans!
Then Ibrox Wanderers in bricht reids an creams,
Parkheid Athletic braw in black an tans,
Culd kick the baw wi neutral sangs an flags.
Till then I juist maun mummle, "Up the Jags".

(poor: pour. clishmaclavers: nonsensical talk.
keech: excrete. ugsome: disgusting. glaikit: stupid.)

XI

A guid Scottis lexicon is warth its wecht
In gowd, as yi fand oot wi Jamieson.
The day we're spilet fur choice. The wirdbuiks on
Oor buirds can lave an auld guy gretlie pecht
Heezin thaim up an doun. It's warth the warsle.
The graith o Scottis wirds we hae tae haun
Cannae be quat in foostie mirk. They maun
Be yaised, kept bricht, set oot as pairt and paircel
O the makaris tuilkist. Ilk wird belangs
No tae yestreen, auldfarrant fowk or wark,
Nor cosh and couthie ingle clash or sangs,
But tae the day, the morn, the haill gret park
O Scotlan in the warld. Oor leid belangs
Tae whamsoe'er can bleeze wi its vital spark.

(wirdbuiks: dictionaries. buirds: shelves. pecht: out of breath.
heezin: hoisting. warsle: effort. graith: treasure. quat: left.
foostie: musty. mirk: darkness. tuilkist: toolbox.
auldfarrant: oldfashioned. cosy: cosy. couthie: sociable.
clash: gossip. leid: language.)

XII

"It's oot frae Davy Lyndsay intae Wallace",
The auld saw hes it, whilk I tak tae mean,
Whit makars tell us in their bauld and gallus
Lines hes virr tae reach the braid demesne
O politics an deeds. Wad it were true!
Aw ower oor land I see a wheen o rhymers,
An some e'en scrievin Scots. Fegs, sic a crew!
The maist their poems are sad wee 'read-wan-timers'
An then 'furget-fur-evers', shilpit straiks
O wurds upo a toom white page, nae set
Nor lilt tae haud the een or lugs, juist fakes
Athoot a passion or a birse, as het
As yestreen's parritch. Whaur are oor trew makars,
Aw thae wha ettle tae be Scotlan-shakars?

(gallus: wild. virr: vigour. wheen: a good few. scrievin: writing.
shilpit: insipid. straiks: streaks. toom: empty. set: form.
athoot: without. birse: anger. ettle: aspire.)

XIII

Sae, Hugh, tell's whit's yir favourite national sang,
Or 'anthem', as they ca' sic cheesy lays?
'Reid Flag' is sae last-century, quite wrang
Fur us the day. I feel 'La Marseillaise'
Is still the best of thaim. Whit maks me boak,
'God Save the Queen', Ma Goad, Goad save us aw,
A Hanoverian jig, a moany joke,
Obsequious whiney wurds tae stap yir craw.
Nae better here fur Scots. Juist 'Scots Wha Hae'
Or 'Flooer o Scotlan', backlins luikin crap.
'Scotlan the Brave', nae fear. Lang syne ae day
Oor Burns sang 'Ça Ira'. Let's hae nae pap.
He bears the gree. Whit better anthem can
Scots sing thegither but 'A Man's a Man'?

(boak: vomit. stap yir craw: cram your throat.
backlins: backward. gree: prize.)

XIV

The staig bestridis its sun-assailin hill,
The laverock singis in its blae lift abune,
The houlet hauntis its mind-deceivin mune,
The thistle rises an forever will.
The eagle spies faur-doun ordainit kill,
The maws snuve ower their sheenin simmer seas,
The wulcat scartis the brainches o its trees,
The thistle rises an forever will.
The adder neath its braken liggs sae still,
The pines aspire ayont their mossie glen,
The hedder spreidis its purpie oan the ben,
The thistle rises an forever will.
The muirs haud doun their saicretis frae the rain,
An aye neath Scotlan's bark its stanes remaine.

(staig: stag. laverock: skylark. houlet: owl. maws: gulls.
snuve: glide. scartis: scratches. liggs: lies.)

XV

Feasgar math, Uisdein, ciamar a tha thu?
You've heard these words in many a Highland mouth.
Ah, but you never had the Gaelic in you,
I was forgetting, you're from the deepest South.
There's a golden wine in the Gaidhealtacht,
And many a cuach's amber bright libation
For you to taste, with "Slainte mhath" and, ach,
You'll need another, just a wee sensation.
Now eisd! The Pinnacle is not accessible
Unless you ken the route. Same with our land.
You'll be needing maps for its unguessable
Surprises. As a bard, you'll understand
Our Alba does surpass its clannish fights
In its remote imaginative heights.

*(feasgar math: good afternoon (evening): Uisdein: Hugh (vocative form):
ciamar a tha thu?: how are you? Gaidhealtacht: Gaelic-speaking area of Scotland.
cuach: drinking cup (quaich). slainte mhath: good health. eisd: listen.)*
(The poem contains echoes of the MacDiarmid poem, "Direadh III")

XVI

I see you, Chris, asprawl upon the beach.
But not just any beach, of course. West Linga.
Where simpler minds might take the chance to fling a
Wee rock into the sea, your thought could reach
Beyond, encompassing geology
And Time and human insignificance
Along this bare raised beach, the dalliance
Of a cold inscrutable tidology.
Your hardest poem strews its words like stones,
Winding its argument like a primeval
Pebble-flow around, beneath, the last upheaval
Of an ebbed sea. Within these northern zones,
On Whalsay now you write and write, the while
Posing for photos, never once a smile?

XVII

Magister/ Hugo/ filius/ Dermotae/ Scotor(um) po/eta
Dactyls and spondees, quantities unmarked,
Imperfectly scanned hexameter from
My long-past Latin class beside the Nith,
Not far from Langholm's Ewes. The Borderland
Is in us both. Later we both were capped,
The same day, you an honoured Doctorate,
Me in my M.A. gown, in Edinburgh.
In Shetland, where I taught, the folk still talked
Of 'Grieves'. So have I followed you about,
Wee man? No, but your poetry follows me.
I share your loves and hates, and celebrate
Or scorn the Scotland of my time, whatever
You make dear. Mad, old, I grieve no more.

Other Scots Poems

Aff tae Istanbul

Aye, its no fur auld guys, this neck ae the wuids,
Aw thae kids eatn each ithers faces,
Haill ae Nature – birds, fish, yi name it –
Gaein at it like rabbits, aw het up
Fur simmer houghmagandie.
Nae time fur their elders, nae manners,
Nae respect, ah tell yi.

Whit can yi expect at my age, ah suppose?
Jist an auld fella livin aff his pension,
Daunerin doon tae the bools an the library.
Wha'll notice yi unless yi stick up fur yirsel?
Aabody else fou ae their ain wind,
Thinkin the licht streams oot their erses.
Onywey, ahm fur offski. Istanbul, here ah come.

Yon wis a smert move aw richt. Use the money
Fae the hoose, get a wee flat in Turkey,
Sea view ae the Bosphorus, Golden Horn like,
Sunshine oan the mosques and domes,
Nae mair pishy Glesca, pits new life intae yi.
Furget aw yi used tae hiv an lost –
It's a new stert, ahm here fur guid an aw.

Yi'll no can recognise me noo, ahm tellin yi.
New fancy gear - yella shirts, cargo pants,
Floppy hat – maks the locals turn thir heids
Fae thir coffee an chat. Aye, yons me noo,
Doon the café oan the dock, haudin forth
Aboot the auld days, state ae the nation,
Me an Wullie Yeats, settin the warld tae richts.

(Ref. W.B. Yeats, "Sailing to Byzantium": "That is no country for old men....") (houghmagandie: sexual relations)

Lady Gray

Early yestreen I walkit oot
Alang the Banks o Cart;
The winter mist frae side tae side
Rowed wi an eldritch art.

The winter mist frae bank tae bank
Spread like a faery moss
Hidin the ford o meikle stanes
Whaur I was bound tae cross.

And mid the stream I saw a maid
In goun an hood o grey,
Her tears ran doon, her bitter croon
Was desolate an wae.

She mourned the deid in mony a sea
Owre aw the warld sae braid,
Smoored in waves an sterved like slaves,
By aw earth's pooers betrayed.

The braken boats that scarce can float,
Stapped fou wi bairns an wives,
Fain tae flee cross the middle sea
Wi monie braken lives.

I heard her keenin rise and faa
For aw puir souls forlorn.
I hear it in my drearie dreams
Frae eventide till morn.

White was the mist on Cart's dark stream,
White was the frost on the brae,
But whitest of aw was the lang lang hair
O banshee Lady Gray.

(Banshee: The Bean Sidhe, the fairy woman,
the weeper at the ford for the dead and those still to die.)

Lykewake Express

("This ae nicht, this ae nicht, every nicht and all,
Fire and fleet and candle-licht, and Christ receive thy sawle.")

"On behalf of ScotRail, welcome aboard this regular evening Border Line service from
Edinburgh Redgauntlet, calling at ...."

It's graun tae hae the auld line back again as
Whan Mither used tae ride it up an doon
Tae Edinburgh on her trips tae Jenners
An shoppin eftirnunes upon the toun.

Tae hae this jaunt doonbye, I'm naethin laith,
Yet, faith, it's no the Border as I mind it.
These stations werenae here, I'll tak my aith.
Aw that I used tae ken, some scoondrel's tyned it.

Whit's Whinnymuir? I ask ye. Thae puir sowls
Skreichin an staggerin owre yon jaggy parks.
Tae see them suffer sae wad melt yir bowels.
An michty me, wha's gane and stole their sarks.

Whit names these places hae! Here's Gurlieburn,
An Corbiedyke, dear God, an Bogleknowe,
Wi Carlincleuch! They mak my stomach turn
An loup wi horror. There's some smert deil's pow

Ahint aw this, or I misdoot mysel',
Cheyngin the gentle Borders that I've kent
Intae an ugsome ante-room o' Hell
Whaur unsuspecting fowk laek me are sent.

Faith, noo, it seems, we've cam tae Brig o' Dreid.
Far doun on either side, I see a sad
Black burn that steams an glows wi streaks o reid.
Yon's no the burn I fished when juist a lad.

We're comin tae the toun at last, thank God,
Whaur sune I'll walk the auld familiar lanes.
Some nichtmare this, mair nor a gey wheen odd.
I'll fair be glad tae rest my weary banes.

"   before arriving at Pitmirkie Central, Low Level, where this service and your journey will finally terminate. Passengers are advised that members of the station staff are on hand to ensure they receive an appropriate reception."

(Edinburgh already has a Waverley Station. A Redgauntlet Station may be appropriate for a new Border line running into the countryside of Walter Scott and the Ballads.)

Donald, Here's to You, Sir

Och, it's yourself, Donald.
Come away in-by and sit you down.
Man, it's a real coarse evening out there.
The snow's low down on the hill – there'll be more
afore the morn's morn, I'll warrant you.
Warm yourself by the stove, get the chill
out of your bones. You'll have a dram?
Aye, aye, a wee drop of the Talisker.
It's no your Lewis craitur, but Skye's near enough.
A wee bit ice? No, just a breath of mist then
to soften the blow. Slainte mhath!
So you've still got the Gaelic, I hear.
Your mother knew how to bring you up well.
Now you're to be the President, it'll serve you fine.
A few words in the Lord's own tongue'll help
to keep thae Senators and Congressmen in order.

My, it'll be a new experience, a real revelation,
for America to have a Leodhasach in charge of things,
bringing the true Highland spirit to your White House
work, having folks in of an evening for a ceilidh,
all sorts, incomers, poor old wifies, all the sick
and needy that the Good Book tells us to look after,
joined together for a dance and songs and stories
in the good old Gaelic way – Aye, that minds me,
my daughter Jean's boy, he's in America now,
driving a New York cab, he's a rare singer,
I can just see you both singing the port-a-beul
together in the ceilidh. Get in touch with him,
Donald. Hussein MacLeod's his name.
See him right. He's family after all.
Och, but your glass is down. Another of the same?

*(A nod in the direction of Donald Trump's Lewis family connection.
The poem is hopefully now of mere historical interest.
port-a-beul: unaccompanied mouth music)*

Saga City

Ah'm shair Ah'll get there, pals, yin day richt suin.
It's juist Ah've been gey thrang, ye ken, wi wark
an aa, the buisness, tryin tae mak ma mark,
the faimly, seein them settled, rinnin roun,
a doolie on the go tae earn a crust.
But noo Ah'm ready, packed an set tae gae.
Ah've got ma sat-nav, read the maps, an sae,
when Ah tak aff, ye'll no see me fur dust.
Ah'm buiked aheid, a nice wee flat, guid view
an near the shops. Imagine drivin through
the dreamin muirs that ligg ahint the toun,
tae reach the gowden burgh neist the sea,
wi squares an prom an central avenue,
the sichts o history, the reasoned soun
o wisdom an guid sense baith fair an free.

Yon's whit sets Saga City ower the lave,
the democratic intellect ahint
the rational discourse, lichtsome wit that's tint
aa malice, passions o the feral cave,
an mental chains. Ah'll dauner by the inns
an clubs tae hear the crack an play o chiels
wha ken ideas row on unchecked wheels
tae gang whaure'er they wull, ower bens or linns,
doun straths o times lang past, or up a corrie
fur glisk o some unscaleit future peak.
Ah'll eat in howffs or causey caffs, an keek
aroun tae see wha's haudin forth. Then, "Sorry,
pal," Ah'll say, "Ah beg tae disagree...."
Sae then Ah'm aff, fair on the wey tae be
a sagamore o guid sagacity.

*Notionally a poem in an occasional sequence called "The Multiple City", which I have
written over the years.*

*(thrang: busy. doolie: witless person. ligg: lie. lave: rest. tint: lost. row: roll. glisk: glance.
howff: a snug bar. causey: pavement.)*

LOBEY DOSSER RYDZ AGEN

Oor hero heidn fur hemm
Lobey rydz acroass the desert
Oan a hoars wi twa legz
Elfie haen a loaty proablemz
SON YA BASS

Lobey ferr needz hiz grub
No a chippy in sicht
Wee guy poapz up wia barra
AIPILS PERRS HON PICT

Wee wify stoapz Lobey
Heidscarfn curlerzn slipprz
Hodn a notis
PERTICK BUS?

Lobey seeza cloody dust
Oot rydz a baddy wia gun
Help ma boab mammy daddy
RANK BAJIN!

AYD WANTIT sez Lobey
Gofer stickz hiz heid ooty a hoal
AL GOFURRIT
Saivd bia wee beesty
Puffy smoak onra hill
Helly aloaty pawneez
Merr oanra wey
OAN YIR BYK BAJIN!

CHEERZ PALZ sez Loaby
Honess injinz aw heidn
Fur Wudlunz anan injin
INGIN BAJIZ IZRA BOAYZ

(in memrio bud neill glesca puntr eckstrordinerr)

The Scottish Patient

(Thou shalt not kill, but needst not strive
Officiously to keep alive.)

"Good morning, nurse, and how's our old friend today?"
"Just the same as aye, doctor, nae better ava."
"And has he had his pills, the soup, to keep the end at bay?"
"Whitever guid it does him, he fair swallies it aa.?

An' then he asks fur mair, faith, sir, the cheek o't.
Yi'd think he'd ken fine weel there's nae restorin'.'"
"Indeed, nurse, palliative care is all that's on the note.
Just keep him ticking over, no more riotous roaring."

"That's richt, he's hid his days o' gie'in us grief,
Wi' his slanjivaws, his camarahashies, hoochs an' skirls.
Yon teuchter langwidj drivin' us aa fair deef.
Time tae mak an end uv aa thae stupid birls and whirls."

"True, nurse, but let's be fair, he's had more than his due
Of loss and sorrow. All his goods, his house and land,
Taken. Who sings his songs or reads his stories? Far too few.
But let's not worry. All is for the best, you understand."

"Shair thing! We're the future, yon auld fule's the past.
It's jist, he still keeps hingin' oan an' cheatin' Daith.
Kin he no dae the decent thing an' dee at last.
Yin fact Ah ken richt weel, there's nae room fur us baith."

The greatest enemies of Gaelic culture and language have
traditionally been in Lowland Scotland.

The Ballad of Archie McGaw

Ye're a fine wee laddie, said Archie McGaw,
Will ye gang tae the wuids wi me?
An I'll shaw ye the tod in his boorie-den
An the whitret ahint the tree.

He went tae the wuids wi Archie McGaw
An he saw the whitret and tod.
The tod cruncht his banes wi sherp white teeth
An the whitret drank his blood.

Ye're a braw young chap, said Archie McGaw,
Will ye climb the bens wi me?
An I'll shaw ye the wullcat in the heather
An the great deer rinnan free.

He clamb the bens wi Archie McGaw
An he saw the wullcat an deer.
The stag gored him deep wi his muckle horns
An the cat clawed him ear tae ear.

Ye're a worthy chiel, said Archie McGaw,
Will ye sail the seas wi me?
An I'll shaw ye the selkie singan her sang
An the haivel's rocky lee.

He sailed the seas wi Archie McGaw
An he saw the conger an seal.
The haivel gruppt him by the throat,
The selkie witcht him in her reel.

Ye're a spry auld man, said Archie McGaw,
Will ye gang doon the pit wi me?
An I'll shaw ye the snake o the nether warld
An the lowes that burn wi glee.

Awa ye gae, foul Archie McGaw,
Ye'll no hae yir sport wi me.
I'm ower canny an wardly wise
Tae be takkin in by yir lee.

He's lifted his stick tae Archie McGaw
An cloured him frae heid tae bum,
Till the black black wizard hae tint his shape
And melted awa up the lum.

*(Archie McGaw: Archimago, a deceitful tempting sorcerer
in The Faerie Queene, by Edmund Spenser.)*

*(tod: fox. boorie-den: lair. whitret: weasel. wullcat: wildcat.
selkie: sealwoman. haivel: conger eel. lowes: fires. lum: chimney.)*

A Guid Scots Education

Maist lernit an esteemit George Buchanan,
Tutor til oor worthie gracious Prince,
Jamy Stewart, heir til oor late remuvit Quene.

I scrieve ye this epistill anent yr charge,
Urgeand that ye spare the rod upo the bairn.
Fearna tae spile him, schaw him luve,

For that he hes na mither that may him cuddle,
An swa he may lue her in filial return
That in his bigger years he may beseik

The Quene Elizabeth she gie her libertie,
That oor Marie may live retirit here
In Scotland wi her faith amang her ain,

Makand na claimes on ony Croon in ony airt.
Swa too meseemis it fit that James hissel
Suld gie up aw his richt til ony forayne realme,

That Englisch may be rewlit by Englisch,
Scottis by Scottis, as fram oor times lang syne,
As oor twa separate pepillis dearly wish.

Oor Scotland needis na tong nor wealth
Nor ony lawis fra Englisch pride.
Her freens hae ever been, an suld

Forever be, across the maine,
In France, in Holland, in Almayne,
Whaur trade an learning flourisch weill.

Last, teiche oor Prince that he suld traist
Na Goddis Richt, nor earl or burgess ainerly,
But turne til puir disprisit Jock the Commonweill,

Wha sall be aye his surest stay an shield.
I scrieve, guid Maister George, this counsell
Fur a future hopefu land under a canny king.
(Schir) Alex Nicol

George Buchanan, the celebrated Scottish scholar and humanist, was appointed as tutor to the future King James VI and I. He was reputed to have been a very severe teacher, beating his pupil cruelly, which may explain a lot about the future king's character.

(meseemis: it seems to me; Almayne: Germany. disprisit: undervalued. Jock the Commonweill: the allegorical figure of the common Scots people.)

A Wearie Fit

They're singan 'Auld Lang Syne'
In Europe's Parliament Ha',
They're linkan tae auld acquaintance
An' Scotlan's gaen awa.

But they dinna ken the hauf ae it,
The auld acquaintance is oot ae mind.
They think that Scotlan's a thing ae the past,
A story that's tauld, a dreme that's dwined.

It's aboot their ain past they should be reidan,
Tales ae historical glory.
They'd find that Scots were aft tae the fore,
A built-in pairt ae thir national story.

French kings' gairds an Baltic traders,
Glesca chiels on the hills ae Spain,
Hielanmen deid at Monte Cassino,
Kilties in Belgium amang the slain.

The guid Schir James wi Bruce's hert
Leadan the Spanish knichts' advance,
Lewis lads wi thir mules in Greece,
Scottish pikemen fechtan for France.11

Wha kens ocht aboot Scotlan
Wha ainly Scotlan kens?
Scotlan is mair nor cities an hills,
Couthie burghs and empty glens.

They're singan 'Auld Lang Syne'
An keepan a lamp alicht.
Gin they really want Scotlan back,
They'll keep it fuelled an bricht.

For we are singan a different sang,
Singan it clearly tae ye.
"We're no awa tae bide awa,
We're gonnae cam back an see ye."

The lands ae Europe, baith great an sma,
We Scots fowk hope tae share,
An the Great Glen ae Europe
Will be traivellt by Scots aince mair.

(linkan: dancing with linked arms. dwined: faded.
couthie: snug)

Whit's in a Name?

Val.
So herr we ur, Holly'n'me, getting oan the plane,
Aff tae the Costa, twa big Glesca lassies
Auld eneuch tae ken better, jeez, shouldae seen wiz,
Burstin oot ae wur straps, cauf length pants,
The maist ae a bottle ae Pinot Grigio sloshin
Inside tae pit wiz in the mood fur apartamento life.
Another great brekk fae the pissiness ae earnin a crust
In the Dear Green Place. See, Holly'n'me gae back a lang wey,
Back tae schuil. Trouble wi Holly, she his a really manky name.
Wad yi believe, Peuf. I kid yi not. Cam fae her German grandad,
Imagine whit she hid tae pit up wi in the playground. And sae
She's keen it his tae be said the proaper wey, Poyf.
No yir average Glesca moniker. Onywey, aff we flee,
Next stop, poolside bar neckin a coupla margaritas. Magic!

Holly.
Trouble wi aw thon vino we hid at Glesca Airport,
We'll be burstin furra pee no lang eftir take-off.
It'll be queuing up the aisle afore we get tae Malaga
An can relax on wur ain balcoany. Then it'll be aff
Doon the toun, check oot the bars an shoe-shops,
Clock the discos fur later in-depth shenanigans, an Val
Bein Val, uv course, stertin tae eye up the visible talent,
Lads oan the hunt thirsels, mibbe a Spanish waiter ur three.
Onything'll dae fur Val. She's cam weill prepared, eneuch fancy
Thongs an things in her case tae kit oot the haill convent.
She'll niver be stuck, can pit oan the real posh as required,
Ms Tringle in her warkin West Endie boutique manner.

Bring it oan, sez I. Herr we ur then, bumpity-bump,
Touch-doon at Malaga. Viva the burdz. España, por favor!

Val Tringle, Holly Peuf – Travelling Hopefully!

Laughing at Confucius

On the Royal Road

They're suspicious of walkers in Colma City.
You get off the train from San Francisco
and start on foot towards the cemeteries.

First you find there are no sidewalks.
As you tread warily between the asphalt
and the weeds, occasional cars speed past

(this not being a major throughway, just the conduit
that leads respectful visitors to the stony forests
of Northern California's dead), and puzzled faces

register your un-American pedestrian nonconformity.
Yet Colma celebrates the un-American, all the departed
securely allocated to their national, cultural

and religious ghettos – Greek and Jewish, Italian,
Serbian (hiding hordes of also-Orthodox Russians)
and more, behind their walled-in exclusivity.

So it goes. And yet, because Memorial Day is near,
their true-American heirs ensure the dead display allegiance,
little Old Glories planted proudly by the artificial flowers.

Our duty done to Babushka, we turn from Katya's
granite slab sharply chiselled in Cyrillic,
make a donation, and step back out into America.

Yet, momentarily, not the same American road,
for, seeing the street sign just across the way,
I realise who were the traffic of the past.

Trains of silver-laden burros, pedlars
and traders, Jesuits from the missions, soldiers,
officials, ladies on horseback, the people of New Spain

and Mexico (as it was before the Yankee robbers),
and all on foot and hoof, up and down
the Royal Road, just as the sign says,

"Camino Real".

Sonnet: On Westminster Bridge, 2017

Earth held not anywhere a fairer scene
Touching the tourists' souls as they passed by
To view a symbol of democracy
And capture it upon a smartphone's screen,
Until, Dear God, a garment of obscene
And indiscriminate atrocity
Falls over all – the maimed and dying lie
In multi-national agony between
The traffic and the river's calm extent.
Ne'er may we in the future quite forget,
After the flowers, the plaque, the silent throng,
How one more place became less innocent,
Less sweet, less glittering, more unsure, though yet
That mighty London heart beats still as strong.

24/03/17

Sonnet on the Departed

Out with you then, off into the sunset,
another victim of the European
Question, slicked-back hair, the man-boobs, derrière,
disguised beneath the Savile Row posh tail-

oring. What after to look forward to?
Consultancies and speeches, five- or six-
figured, channelled into offshore holdings,
maybe a peerage, chancellor of a cash-

strapped varsity. But as the temples grey,
the chickens squawk their homeward course to roost.
Those boxes from the Eastern shambles mock
your awkward reverence, opened archives spill
the beans, the music finally is faced,
and failure, failure, scents your evening air.

Touché, Touché!

This week I shall be mostly into inappropriate touching.
Monday.
Touch my cap, touch my toes,
Tap me on the shoulder and hold my nose.
Tuesday.
My Midas touch goes everywhere,
Touch me for a tenner if you dare.
Wednesday.
A touch of the flu', a touch of the jitters,
Time for a gin with a touch of bitters.
Thursday.
I shall, touch wood, be a touchstone of sobriety,
Call in the touch judge in case of dubiety.
Friday.
In the course of my usual eloquent natter
I shall touch upon many a topical matter.
Saturday.
If I touch the hem of your garment,
It's a fitting gesture without any harm meant.
Sunday.
Long gone are the days of the double-declutch,
Alas, I seem to be losing my touch.

Only a game

Welcome to Brexit

the show that puts

obscure ignorance to the test

It used to be called

Pointless

We asked umpteen million people

what they knew about Europe

Fewer than 40% said "Nothing"

to the head-to-head

Now you can confer

How many types of European can you name?

Krauts, frogs, dagoes, wops, polacks, olafs,

Johnny Foreigner!

Wins you the pointless trophy

You have fought off all the competition

Now you can go for the crackpot

****

Unfortunately you have not found

that all-important pointless answer

Wins you nothing

Sends you off home – alone

Echoes in the caves of Albion

"Brussels bureaucrats try every trick to paralyse
                    (*Echo:* "Lies")
Our British freedom, tie us down with foreign traces,
                    (*Echo:* "Racists")
Grab our jobs, our wealth, in greedy handfuls.
                    (*Echo:* "Fools")
We'd truthfully do better profiting by trade
                    (*Echo:* "Betrayed")
With all the world instead. Let's leave, free men,
                    (*Echo:* "Remain")
And make our Dear Old England great at last.
                    (*Echo:* "Alas!")
A richer brighter future lies ahead of us in lieu."
                    Echo: "E.U......Eheu!)

Back in the Tang Dynasty

Back in the Tang it was all jade:
Jade earrings, hairpins, danglies, cups,
Lutes and zithers, for heaven's sake,
Vases, dishes, tigers, boats, you name it.
People and places: beautiful Green Jade
The concubine, Jade Flower the Emperor's horse,
Jade City, the Jade Gate Pass, Jade Mountain.
'I am the madman of Chu with my green jade staff,
Laughing at Confucius.'

Charlie's Pep Talk

(or, Laughing All the Way to the Grouse Moor)

Right, people, listen up. It's time to down
Your g. and t's and Pimms. Forget the frown.
Remember who we are. The Firm's in town.

Let's get out there. The Balcony awaits.
Tourists and loyal subjects throng the gates.
It's Mumsies's birthday. Britain celebrates.

You know the drill, just where you have to stand,
Although the problem's getting out of hand.
The swelling of our fertile royal band

Means that it's going to be like whiffy socks
Out there, with bulgy suits and frocks
Rubbing on tums and boobs and beefy hocks,

And prickly uniforms all pressed together
In this too seasonable summer weather.
We'll smell of rankness and Imperial Leather.

But come on, people, no more poohs and yahs,
Sprogs to the front to prompt the oohs and ahs,
And, well up front, we need the Mas and Pas.

So, gels, collect your charges from the Nanny.
You'll find they've been cleaned up from mouth to fanny,
Well-sanitised in every nook and cranny.

Your gloves won't suffer. You can wave quite freely.
Lads, just look manly. It's quite simple, really.
Think of your fancy swords, be stern and steely.

As for you quasi-royal odds and sods
Left over, stand behind like stookie rods,
Make with the smiles, the gracious waves and nods.

While all the older guys just stick with me,
Stand round Mama in solidarity,
Windsor United for all the world to see.

Down in the yard a redcoat band will play,
Some cannon fire off blanks quite far away,
And overhead some ageing planes display

Three cloudy trails of red and white and blue.
So now step lively, chaps, keep smiling through.
Remember this is what we're paid to do.

Don Roberto's Europe.

Lunched in the Art Club last week, met this old guy,
Big beard, lots of hair, talking pretty posh.
He told me stories about his time in Paris when he was young,
Rode his horse along the Bois de Boulogne,
Met an actress and married her, hobnobbed with artists
And writers, Goncourts, De Maupassant, the whole shebang,
Theatre, restaurants, salons, demi-monde, you name it.
   A far cry from Bath Street, if you ask me.

Back at the Club one evening, the old fellow was there again.
Told him about my timeshare on the Costa, that set him off,
Couldn't shut him up, got the whole spiel
About his Spanish Granny, staying with her family on the Med,
Riding horses all over the campo, speaking the lingo like a true Pedro,
Living up north in Vigo with his missus, knowing counts and dukes
And other toffs, looking for gold (no luck there), chewing the fat
With diplomats and anarchists, Madrid, Barcelona, Burgos, wherever,
Doing the real hidalgo bit, with a touch of the common man.
   Really put my two-week package at a peep.

Saw him the other day again, up in the old Billiard Room,
Looking lost, *Where have they put the cues and tables?*
Mentioned my City Break in Rome, started him off again,
The Eternal City, legions of true Italian peasants,
A posh Roman lady-friend he'd dedicated a book to,
Sidestepping to Portugal, what a fine place was Lisbon,
He'd seen the Emperor of Brazil there once on the street
(The What? Of Where? Come on!), great fiestas and weddings,
The lost King Sebastian, more horses, of course, must have them.
   That man could write a Thomson's brochure.

Lots of chit-chat at other meetings, Germany, the Baltic,
He'd seen them all, South America too, all over,
Not forgetting Morocco just across the Straits, until I found
He actually hailed from a place upby, close by Drymen
where my auntie used to bide, *Now you're talking,* I says,
Who needs Europe when you can have the Trossachs,
No place like dear old Scotland?
   Thought I had him there, cut his big talk down to size.

He laughs and strokes his beard, off he goes again,
What know they of Scotland who only Scotland know?
A poet I know said that but he was talking about England.
Alba of the warriors, Caledonia stern and wild,
Scotia Land of Cakes and Usquebaugh, all the self-flattering fictions
To make you believe you're more than a bit of padding
Round England's waist. Europe, you'll never be apart from it.
You have been, are and always will be a part of it.
   Here, here, I says, what about Britain, don't knock it.

The old guy makes his way to the Club door, turns and says,
Scotland in Europe is older than a poor wee Scotland stuck inside
This tarnished British mirror to England's vanity.
These racialists can try to drag Scotland out of Europe,
But they can never take Europe out of Scotland,
I should know, amigo, sangre y huesos,
Blood and bones. And now excuse me,
My steed awaits. And out he went,
   Last I saw of him, him and his horses indeed,
   Good riddance.

Haibun

Rossetti's Dream.

The poet walks in Willow Wood. Knights and ladies
haunt his mind, red hair spilling over the artist's hands,
Ophelia's face beneath the water, Romantic myths.

By the pool, a youth weeps with Love at his shoulder. His
tears dimple the surface; cold skin, blue eyes, pale lips
look up in shivers, reflecting a medieval sky.

Love sings to the ghosts under the leaning trees, "All ye
who walk in Willow Wood...."

willow leaves
speckle a window
obscure each face's view

Hemispheric

LEFT	RIGHT
as I had indeed	predictably
been told	no excuses
it was a monastery	spared by reformers
and yes there were	cucumber sandwiches
brothers in robes	preserved their silence
to be seen	you have to wave
here and there	wherever you go
mainly of course	there were beer-gardens
it was a gasthaus	frequented by burly thugs
my room	with a view
is germanically	perhaps too formal
immaculate	conceptions are rare
the tilt and turn	in a feathered hat
windows	opening to a newer world
were new to me	I was an innocent
in the 1990s	before technology
the evening meal	nostalgia for simplicity
left much	on my plate of life
to be desired	beauty is required
soup with bread	every day without fail
cold meats cheese	it's a picnic
and herbal tea	rain is to be expected
no bar	to my ambitions
within the holy	ever upwards
precincts	of an active mind
but yet a brother	not yet lost to me
sat just inside	outside downside
the back door	into Arcadia
selling German beer	fragrant blossoming
in bottles	by a lichened well
at two euros each	could be worse
a brisk walk	clearing the sinuses
through a frosting garden	opening the pores
in a Rhineland chill	oh for the moon
and back to my	inconstant shining
monastic cell	among the stars
with two glass	indifferent eyes
companions for the night	forever disappointed
at breakfast	bring forth the day
a brawny brother	twitching my mantle blue
demanded money	tomorrow to fresh woods
with a hint of menace	smile boys smile
to pay the cost	the piper at the gates
of a midnight	of dawn
phone call home	auf wiedersehen pet

Poppies No More

(11th November 2018)

Donny and Alick, I keep your medals
Safe in a plastic box,
No 'Distinguisheds', just General Service,
Like so many other Jocks.

Great-uncles and brothers, I never knew you,
So cannot remember aught
Except that long before my time
You went to France and fought

And there you died. I have seen your names
In the National Honour Rolls.
For years your family wore their poppies
Like millions of mourning souls.

Along came another instalment of war
With Herr Hitler calling the shots.
More of the family answered the call
As patriotic Scots.

Thus once more they were forced to join
The ultimate enterprise,
And Highland uncle, Canadian cousin,
Fell to death from the skies.

You too, my father, spared from the First,
Saw the summons to duty beckoning.
Middle-aged overworked heavy smoker,
The Home Guard brought your reckoning.

Ever since, in pride of remembrance,
I have done my November bit,
Observed the silence, worn the poppy,
Been the expected Brit.

(11 a.m.)
I write these words in two minutes of silence
That fill this annual space.
What is it that I can truly remember?
Only my father's face.

Real remembrance counts no more.
It's replaced by a plastic emotion.
The blood of the poppy has long dried up.
Red bile is the current potion.

The poppied slopes of Afghanistan
And the blooms of Flanders field
Provide their equally potent drugs
For profiteers to wield.

Red poppies serve our political masters,
A subtle exertion of power.
Remembrance is now a military tool
And war is excused by a flower.

Dissent is lulled to acceptance,
Anger's bereft of its pain,
Poppies adorn the recruiting drive,
Young men can be redcoats again.

While the Poppy-Fascists go out and about
Hounding the poppyless every day,
And poppies become the loyalty card
For a right-wing Brand UK.

So, since I have come to maturest years
On the brink of eighty-four,
I know my mind, I see things plain,
I shall wear poppies no more.

Stendhal on a Spanish Balcony

A close-knit peloton toils up the slope
Past Avalon, helmets and lycra,
Muscled legs straining. Cars behind
Stack up until the roundabout
At Paraiso lets some through to head
At speed to Torrox and Velez Malaga.

Clear out to sea. Three windsurfers
Dip and rise between the grey furrows
Of a sun-deserted Med. Inland,
Above the fractured peaks, clouds mass
And mists creep in to warn of evening
Chill and rain. Mid-March in the South.

I'm getting seriously pissed off with Fabrizio.
No sooner does he emerge from one arrest,
Imprisonment, assault unscathed, to take up
With another maid or actress, singer
Or heiress, but off he dashes, false
Passport at the ready, to repeat his folly.

Between the Marinas de Nerja overflow
Car-park and Paraiso's chiringuito
Sprawls a tolerated shanty-land of unspoiled
Andalusia – thatched-roof cabana,
Donkey-shed, hen-houses, overgrown
Grazing and free-range fenced-in enclosure.

Two donkeys wander to and fro, a dozen hens
Pace and flutter when the inshore
Wind abates. The cockerel proclaims his mastery
At intervals from dawn till dusk. No sign
Of human life – whoever's there behind
The shutters, long may he avoid developers' grip.

Neo-classic realist that he was, Stendhal
Attributed a skill in rational discourse to all
His characters – at least to the aristocrats.
Being French, yet Bonapartist, no doubt he saw
This trait as natural. So every lengthy
Chapter sees one or more of these counts

Or duchesses or well-bred maidens, Fabrizio
Too of course, withdraw into a kind of cloister
Of the mind to ruminate upon their situation
Within a complex plot – not so much a stream
Of consciousness in Joycean style,
More of a Ciceronian oration to the Senate.

The sea glitters this morning over to Africa.
The day of wind is in the past, this is a now
Of broken hollow stems above the watermark.
On the far horizon two container ships
Pass eastward to an improbable Levant
Over the shipless sparkle of an empty Med.

And that is all. Where are the coasters and the tramps,
All they who once went down in ships to sea?
The Middle Sea has been abandoned. Yet some
Are being expected and awaited. Two choppers
On patrol go clattering west, keeping Spain's eye
Alert for leaky boats freighted with Africa's despair.

Notes — An Altitude Within

1   There is, of course, no Gaelic original to this supposed translation.
2   People from the Lochcarron district of Ross and Cromarty.
3   Pronounced 'Sgayr Chrackach' approximately): islet in Loch Carron, meaning 'craggy rock'. 'ch' pronounced as in 'loch'
4   Pronounced 'awp' approximately).'A land-locked bay', the bay in front of Dal a'Chladaich, a group of houses on the north shore of Loch Carron, west of Lochcarron village.
5   Pronounced 'Sgayr Ahta' approximately): islet in Loch Carron, meaning 'long rock'. 'ch' pronounced as in 'loch'
6   Duncan, Janet.
7   Janet.
8   The three Isles of Crowlin are situated off the coast of Applecross in Wester Ross.
9   chair *(Gaelic)*
3   Red is a significant colour in traditional ballads.
4   The poem is in 'terza rima' form.
5   There is, of course, no Spanish original to this supposed translation.
6   *"What country, friends, is this?....."* (Shakespeare, *Twelfth Night*, Act I, Sc.2).
7   While London was getting to grips with the July 2005 bombings, the international Island Games were being held in Shetland.
8   The poem is written in sixteenth-century Scots in the form of a double sonnet, as practised by James VI and I and his "Castalian Band" of Scottish court poets.
9   The reference is to James Leslie Mitchell (Lewis Grassic Gibbon), author of the novel, *Sunset Song*, who served for a time in the British Army in what is now Iraq just after the First World War.
10 A ghazal is a verse form in Arabic poetry.
    The poem contains references to the poetic drama, *Hassan*, by James Elroy Flecker.
11 Literary references are to Hugh MacDiarmid, Alasdair Gray, Edwin Morgan and Robert Cunninghame Graham.
12 Charles Trenet, French singer and song-writer, composer of "La Mer".
    "Depuis que les bals sont fermés", a song performed by the French chanteuse, Damia.
13 The film, *The Thief of Bagdad*, produced by Alexander Korda (1940) starred Conrad Veidt as Jaffar and Sabu as Abu, the thief.
14 The film, *Blade Runner*, directed by Ridley Scott (1982) was made from the novel, *Do Androids Dream of Electric Sheep?* (1968), by Philip K.Dick.
15 The widespread practice of forced marriage is fully documented on the Internet.
16 The Battle of Culloden (1746) involved Scots on both sides.
    The Hanoverian army contained many Lowland Presbyterians, who regarded the Highland Catholics and Episcopalians with deep hatred.
17 The poem makes use of images of the execution of Mary Queen of Scots.
18 The tragedy of Princess Diana is the pure stuff of traditional ballad.
19 "Chicago Sam" is Sam Giancana, the head of the Chicago Mafia.
20 Sir Roger is a stuffed elephant, a longstanding exhibit at the Glasgow Kelvingrove Museum and Art Gallery.
21 These next five poems are translations into Scots of Pablo Neruda love-sonnets from *Cien Sonetos de Amor*.
22 Another poem in "terza rima" form.

23	A memory of wartime childhood in Dumfries.
24	A 'fabliau' is a mediaeval French story form, often dealing with a sexually improper subject.
25	Kilgore Trout is a recurring figure in the satirical fiction of Kurt Vonnegut, Jr.
26	The late Ian Hamilton Finlay, poet, sculptor and landscape gardener, wrote a brilliant little book in the Glasgow dialect, *glesca beasts and a burd, wi, aw, some inseks an, haw, a fush.*
27	Brian Osborne was a fine scholar and librarian who did much research into the life and works of the Scottish author and journalist, Neil Munro. Brian died on holiday in Central Asia and is buried near Samarkand. The sonnet contains references to Munro's novels and stories.
28	The poem is an double abecedarian, i.e., a poem of 26 lines beginning A-Z in order, and ending with z-a.
29	The haibun is a Japanese form comprising a brief imaginative prose section and one or more haiku.
30	An eclogue is a pastoral dialogue, originally involving shepherds and shepherdesses. The inspiration here is the English Renaissance poem, "The Passionate Shepherd to his Love" by Christopher Marlowe.
31	Robert Bontine Cunninghame Graham, explorer, politician and writer, was present at the dedication of the memorial to his friend, Neil Munro, only months before his death in his beloved Argentina.

Notes — fnc gull

Opinions and emissions of fnc gull.

I

1   "The Raven", Edgar Allan Poe.
2   The poet, Edwin Morgan, lived for many years in the Anniesland district of Glasgow. He wrote a poem about a seagull that came to a window of his flat.
3   *Macbeth*, William Shakespeare.
4   *The Scarlet Pimpernel*, Baroness Orczy.

II

5   Times change and we change with them.
6   *Twelfth Night*, William Shakespeare.
7   The houses painted in different colours along the sea front in Tobermory, Mull, were used in the BBC children's TV series, "Balamory".

III

8   The Prime Minister, Gordon Brown.
9   A sonnet by William Wordsworth.
10   Architectural features on the Scottish Parliament building.

IV

11   In 2006 the football World Cup finals were held in Germany.
12   References to the Glasgow football clubs, Celtic, Rangers and Partick Thistle respectively.

V

13   The words spoken by General Douglas MacArthur on receiving the Japanese surrender in August, 1945, effectively ending the Second World War.
14   Away up in the sky, a catchphrase of the Scots comedian, Dave Willis.
15   Referring to both the poem, "Crowdieknowe", by Hugh MacDiarmid and the novel, Cloud Howe, by Lewis Grassic Gibbon.
16   "The Bonnie Broukit Bairn", Hugh Mac Diarmid.
17   "America the Beautiful", Katherine Lee Bates.
18   "Canedolia", Edwin Morgan.
19   The Gaelic area of Highland Scotland.
20   Words supposedly spoken by General MacArthur on suffering an initial defeat by the Japanese in World War II.

The travels and further effusions of fnc gull...

I

21   "The Star-Spangled Banner".
22   Gaelic for the Land of Youth, out to the west ac cording to Gaelic legend.

II

23   "Elegy XIX. On His Mistress Going to Bed", John Donne.

24   "I have nothing to declare but my genius", said by Oscar Wilde on entering the USA.

25   The Statue of Liberty in New York Harbour was presented to the USA by the people of France in 1886 as a mark of friendship..

26   Ref. Uncle Sam, the national stereotype of the USA.

27   "Give me your tired, your poor, your huddled masses...", words inscribed on the pedestal of the Statue of Liberty.

III

28   Ref. "the topless towers of Ilium", *Dr Faustus*, Christopher Marlowe.

29   Adam Smith, Scottish philosopher and econo mist, author of *The Wealth of Nations*.

30   Gaelic greeting, "How are you?"

IV

31   "Landing of the Pilgrim Fathers", Mrs Felicia Hemans.

32   A story by Richard Bach (1970), a hippie allegorical fable.

33   Derived from "Cloodigowkburgh" in Douglas Young's Scots translation of *The Birds* by Aristophanes, where it is Cloud Cuckoo Land, a bird heaven.

V

34   A play by Eugene O'Neill.

35   *Four Quartets*, "Little Gidding" T.S. Eliot.

VI

36   Expensive sporting shotguns.

37   An area of the city of Inverness beside the sea.

VII

38   Henry VIII, William Shakespeare.

39   "Ulysses", Alfred Lord Tennyson.

40   *A Winter's Tale*, William Shakespeare.

41   "The Rolling English Road", G.K. Chesterton.

Notes — Redomones

1   Inspired by fragments of a Norse ballad, now called *The Hildina Ballad*, written down in 1774 by the Rev. George Low from the reciting of an old Foula man, William Henry. It was in the Norn tongue, the form of Norse spoken in Shetland down to the eighteenth century. The Norn original and a translation by W.G. Collingwood can be found *in A Shetland Anthology*, edited by J.J. and L.I. Graham, 1998.

2   Scottish Ballad refs. in sequence: *Sir Patrick Spens; The Wife of Ushers Well; The Demon Lover; Tam Lin; Thomas the Rhymer (True Thomas)*.

3   2011 marked the 30th anniversary of the publication of the novel, *Lanark*, by Alasdair Gray. Key motifs in the novel are: John Bunyan's *The Holy War*, the structure of the Greek Epic; and Thomas Hobbes' *Leviathan*.

4   As an 85th birthday tribute from Glasgow to the poet Edwin Morgan, the Scots Makar, 85 admirers of his work read their chosen poems of his for a presentation CD. This poem describes the experience of reading the sonnet, "A Golden Age", from Morgan's "Sonnets from Scotland". The quotation in the first line and the last two lines refer to this sonnet.

5   The title alludes to the poet Edwin Morgan, who died in August, 2010. The poem is intended to celebrate the imaginative range and versatility of his poetic achievement.

6   2010 was the centenary of the birth of the poet, Norman MacCaig. 'Maighstir' is the Gaelic word for Master.

7   The literary achievement of the Scottish writer, Neil Munro, is likened to the variety and stature of a Munro, the tallest category of Scottish mountain.

8   Callanish, with its ring of ancient stones, is on the Isle of Lewis.

9   J.T. was a pupil I taught many years ago at Annan Academy. The poem deals with an experience that very many teachers will recognise.

10   This poem is, like the two that follow, an elegy in memory of a dear friend and colleague. Joe O'Neill was not only a fine teacher but also a Latin and Irish Gaelic scholar. The quotation is from Horace's Odes Book I, XXII: *"The honourable man, free from vice, does not require Moorish darts or bow...."*

11   James Inglis was a formidable scholar and teacher, deeply committed to excellence and social causes.

12   Ref. Frank O'Hara and his New York poems. Donald Dewar was the first First Minister of the Scottish Parliament, too soon and abruptly lost to the nation. His statue stands outside the Glasgow Royal Concert Hall.

13   *Lord of the Dance*. James Muir was loved by all, an enthusiast for language and books, a dedicated writer of stories and poetry. His funeral was deeply moving, made all the more so by its use of the John Barry music from the film "Dances with Wolves".

14   Many Scottish people, including Highlanders, found their way to South America and a variety of new lives.

15   The over-building and commercialisation of the south of Spain is a phenomenon of the last three decades, destroying many of the features that made it so appealing to visitors from the rest of Europe.

16   The Scots language of this translation of the first part of Pablo Neruda's *Barcarola* (*Residencia en Tierra*, 1935) is in a traditional literary mode.

17   Garcilaso de la Vega (c.1501-1536) was a Spanish soldier, courtier and poet, a Renaissance figure rather like Sir Philip Sidney in England, who died young fighting against the French. In his short life he wrote poetry in various forms, notably a sequence of forty sonnets in which he explored the pains and frustrations of love.

18   This was commissioned in 2011 by Comrie Development Trust as an inscription for a standing stone to be erected at the new Cultybraggan Heritage Centre beside the village. The stone was chosen and carved by Robbie Schneider.

19   This was composed as a first draft of a possible inscription for a stone to be placed in a sculpture garden. The idea was inspired by the Greek myth of Sisyphus and is an ongoing project with Robbie Schneider.

20   This was commissioned by the Association for Scottish Literary Studies to accompany their annual award of Honorary Fellowships for services to Scottish Literature.

21   This poem was written for the Big Burns Supper Event Competition in Dumfries, January, 2012. It was publicly displayed on a window-pane in the Globe Inn on the High Street.

22   How a teacher may be reincarnated to suit each turn of educational fashion.

23   The Gainsborough portrait of the Honourable Mrs Graham is in the National Gallery of Scotland in Edinburgh. It was painted between 1775 and 1777 when Mary Cathcart (the second daughter of the Earl of Cathcart) was newly married to Thomas Graham of Balgowan. At the time of the portrait, she was in her teens. In 1788 she met Robert Burns at the home of her brother-in-law, the Duke of Athole, at Blair Castle, and Burns described her in a letter as "beautiful Mrs Graham". She contracted tuberculosis and died in 1792 aged thirty-five. Her grief-stricken husband had the portrait put in a case and stored in a London picture-framer's back room. He went on to have a distinguished military career, becoming one of Wellington's generals in Spain and Portugal, and gaining the title of Earl of Lynedoch. He lived on to the age of ninety-six, and after his death in 1843, his heir bequeathed the portrait to the National Gallery of Scotland on the condition that it should never leave Scotland.

24   A memory of a lost Golden Age of Hollywood.

25   Ref. the detective novels of Raymond Chandler.

26   *Croque-monsieur* is a toasted sandwich of ham and cheese.

27   Incidental reference is made at the end to the film, *The Wicker Man*.

28   In *The Lord of the Rings* and *The Hobbit*, the orcs were dealt a really bad hand. With proper dental care and dietary advice, their image could have been much more positive.

29   POTUS is President of the United States. The Kennedy/West Wing pose in silhouette is now a cliché of the office.

30   The book, *The Democratic Intellect*, is essential reading for anyone seeking to make educational policy for Scotland.

31   A personal memory of June, 1953.

32   A neat visual trick by our non-political BBC, reducing Scotland by one third of its real area.

33   The more I revisit this poem, the more it seems to me to be about politics than about a failing personal relationship.

34   A compendium of all the physical abuses visited upon women in this male-dominated world.

35   The seasonal creep associated with climate change has produced some bizarre effects.

36   The local references are personal and mostly Scottish.

Notes — Eye to the Future

1   This poem sequence of fourteen poems was written during the run-up to and the immediate aftermath of the 2014 Scottish independence referendum. Fortune's whirligigs and Time's revenges have made some of them appear already dated and others more relevant. However, they capture some of the attitudes and feelings that were widely on display in Scotland at the time. The concrete poem on the title-page plays with the words in Scots, English, Gaelic, Spanish and Catalan for "eye", "always", "yes", "I", "there is" and "future".

2   "Better Together" was the slogan of the No Campaign in the referendum.

3   "Right" has always been David Cameron's favourite word.

4   Personal memories from primary school.

5   A popular television series, *Borgen*, brought Danish politics, with its interesting parallel possibilities, to Scottish attention.

6   During the referendum campaign, the Spanish Prime Minister, mindful of the relevance to Catalonia, expressed hostility to the idea of Scottish independence. After the death of King Robert the Bruce, the 'Good' Sir James Douglas placed his heart in a casket and took it with him on crusade. In Spain he joined in a campaign against the Moors in Granada, and died fighting in battle, following Bruce as he had often done in the past. During the Spanish Civil War, many Scots joined the International Brigade. They are remembered by a statue in Glasgow of the notable Spanish Communist leader, 'La Pasionaria'.

7   La Diada: the Catalan National Day. At five o'clock in the afternoon of the 11th September, 2013, 400,000 Catalans joined hands to form "una cadena humana", a human chain, the length of Catalonia from the French border in the north to the Province of Valencia in the south. A further 1.6 million demonstrators for a Catalan Independence referendum came out on the streets of Barcelona.

8   Despite the apparent defeat of the Yes Campaign, it continued to flourish and grow, until, in May of 2015, the Scottish National Party obtained a near total victory in the General Election in Scotland.

9   An image of a speculative future. The last line refers obliquely to the Great Tapestry of Scotland, which has been on display in various Scottish locations. There is a reference to W.H. Auden in the first sonnet section: "History to the defeated may say Alas/but cannot help or pardon."

Notes — Riding to Trapalanda

1   This poem was written as an exercise in the use of the subjunctive in Spanish. The structure is based on a poem by the Nicaraguan poet, Ernesto Cardenal. My original (in some respects faulty) Spanish version, *La Pasión de Don Roberto*, has been scrutinised and improved by Robin Cunninghame Graham and Maria Cuerdo Estorga. John C. McIntyre has created an alternative Spanish version.

2   In his writings, Robert Cunninghame Graham frequently mentions Trapalanda, the lost mythical city of the Indians of the pampas, a haven for horses. Graham was a personal friend of some of the artists of the Glasgow Boys school, including John Lavery and Joseph Crawhall ("Creeps"). The wild horses of the pampas ran in herds, or troops (tropillas), rounded up as needed by the Argentine Gauchos, like Exaltación Medina and Raimundo Barragán, friends of Graham in the 1870s. Gartmore was the large Cunninghame Graham estate and house in Menteith, which had to be sold in 1900 because of debts. "Chid" was Graham's nickname for his wife Gabriela, who died in 1906.). The poem was written for and read at the 2014 Annual Dinner of the Cunninghame Graham Society.

3   In his short story, "At the Ward Toll", Robert Cunninghame Graham imagines riding through the mist one night near his old house of Gartmore in the Vale of Menteith and meeting a Spanish seaman, Ildefonso Lopez, making his way to find a ship at Glasgow. They talk briefly and part. The poem imagines the encounter from Lopez' point of view. The poem was written for the 2018 McCash Scots Poetry Competition.

4   Although descended from the Earls of Menteith and Robert III King of Scots, Robert Cunninghame Graham was a dedicated Radical and Socialist both in and out of Parliament. The poem imagines what a brief reign of King Robert might have been like. The poem was published in *The Herald* to mark the inaugural meeting of the Cunninghame Graham Society in 2013.

5   The Spanish word for 'Hopes'. The life and achievement of the Scottish traveller, writer and politician, Robert Bontine Cunninghame Graham, is at last being recognised. On the night before the burial of his wife, Gabriela, on the Isle of Inchmahome in the Lake of Menteith, Robert Cunninghame Grahame dug her grave himself, assisted by one of his old tenants. On its completion, he sat in the Abbey ruins and smoked a cigarette in accordance with her wishes. Thirty years later he was laid beside her. The poem was written for the McCash Scots Poetry Competition, and was published in *The Smeddum Test* (Kennedy & Boyd, 2013), a collection of winning and commended poems from the competition.

6   On the occasion of the dedication of the Neil Munro Memorial in Glen Aray beside Inveraray, 28th June, 1935, Graham was a member of the official part. He was a speaker and praised the achievement of his friend, Neil Munro. This was fully reported in the local press at the time, and the poem is wrong to suggest otherwise. *Mea culpa*. The poem was first published in *ParaGraphs*, the bulletin of the Neil Munro Society.

7   Written for the unveiling of a memorial plaque to 'Don Roberto' at the Lake of Menteith, 07/09/17, and published in *The Herald* on that day. It was later translated into Spanish by Graham's great-grand-nephew, Robin Cunninghame Graham of Gartmore and María Cuerdo Astorga, to whom the poet is indebted for permission to include it here.

8   This is a pure flight of fancy, inspired by a vision of a President Graham, who would be a total antithesis of President Trump in every political stance and utterance. It was written for and delivered at the 2017 Annual Dinner of the Cunninghame Graham Society.

Notes — Walking to the Island

1   The river of cairns

2   The informal term for a member of the Free Presbyterian Church.

3   Little green hill.

4   Janet.

5   Field on the Shore, Shore Meadow

6   Charles

7   A keepen, a tether, usually for a cow, consisting of an iron peg in the ground, to which the animal is attached by a chain or a rope, allowing it a restricted area for grazing.

8   Murdo's woman or wife.

9   You little hero.

10   Old woman

11   A bay.

12   A town in Switzerland, on Lake Maggiore, where in 1925 a series of international pacts was agreed, hopefully guaranteeing peace in Western Europe.

13   Boy, when being directly addressed.

14   A fantasy novel, one of a series written by Edgar Rice Burroughs.

15   A little boy.

16   Who are you?

17   Alan, boy (a direct address)

18   Johnny, Kenny's son.

19   The wife of Alasdair.

20   People of Lochcarron

21   The port of the boundary. It used to mark the boundary between Bruaich in Slumbay and Rhu Dhu (Blackpoint).

22   Land of Youth

23   The name of a house standing on its own up the hill behind Slumbay, probably named by someone who had once lived in South America.

24   grandson

25   A mansion just outside Inverness. The site is now occupied by Raigmore Hospital.

26   The largest of three small islands off the Applecross peninsula, to which some families were cleared in the earlier nineteenth century.

27   Good afternoon, good evening.

28   Good night.

Notes — Insular Poems

1   King George V, died 1936.
2   Kirkcaldy in Fife.
3   During the Second World War, a large tract of the West Highlands was designated a 'Prohibited Area' for special wartime activities like Commando training and convoy monitoring. Special passports were needed by people wishing to visit family members resident in the area. These passports were checked by military personnel at stations on the Inverness-Kyle railway line.
4   'Hill of Mist'. The local name for the hill, Glas Bheinn, behind Lochcarron village.
5   Getulio Vargas, later dictator of Brazil. After World War II, some South American republics, not unreasonably, tried to stop the large outflow overseas of profits made by foreign-owned businesses.
6   One of a series of stories about a Spanish aristocratic brigand. Perhaps the beginning of a lifelong interest in Hispanic culture and the Spanish language.
7   The start of my formal Spanish studies, at Dumfries Academy.

Index

42 George Street, Dumfries, 1937-41 274
A Daily Walk through History 290
A Distant Guitar 271
A Good Day for Mr Pepys 170
A Guid Scots Education 318
A Hero of the New World 158
A Lear of the Suburbs. 169
A New Kind of Hero 10
A Seasonal Catalogue 3
A Wearie Fit 320
Aff tae Istanbul 308
Afterbirth 267
Alphabeat 100
American Cross Code 184
An Altitude 64
An Altitude Within 1
An t-Eilean Sliombagh (The Island) 256
Anger 152
Aye, Man, Aye 230
Back Gardening by Numbers 83
Back in the Tang Dynasty 330
Barcos en el Lago 242
Battle Site 46
BBC Weather Map 205
Beannachd Leibh (Goodbye, and Blessings on You) 260
Beltane 178
Better Thegither 218
Big Guy on the Town 156
Black and White 2
Boats on the Lake 241
Boatsang 160
Brian Splendid 98
By the Way 110
Callanish 150

Camelot Vignette 54
Carranaich 12
Catcall 213
Cathair 15
Changing Guard 99
Character 8
Charlie's Pep Talk 331
Chinese New Year in Kelvingrove 56
Class Outline 185
Class Photo, 1943 277
Cockcrow 167
Coming Ashore 25
Creationists Ahoy! 192
Croque Monsieur 176
Crowlin Mor 13
Cunning Plan for Honourable Victory 102
Cycle Puncture 209
Dail a' Chladaich (The Shore Meadow) 248
Day on the Hill 149
Dear 5A Classmates, 44
Departing 22
Do Photos Dream of Paper Birds? 41
Dominus Reconstructus 168
Don Roberto's Europe. 333
Donald, Here's to You, Sir 312
Easter Poem 38
Echoes in the caves of Albion 329
Eclogue – In The Gallery 104
Elegy on some Gentlemen of Fortune 173
Endangered Species 106
Esperanzas 239
Eye to the Future **217**
Fabliau 90
Fashion Notes 48
Feli City 69
Fero City 68

First Day, 1940   275
Firth of Clyde   34
Flower Power   23
for ever   4
Forebodings   7
Foresters' Arms, January, mid-1950s   291
Four Sonnets of Garcilaso de la Vega   161
from Two Native Lands — A Love Song   21
From a Distance   85
From the Gaelic   11
From the Pictish Phrase-book   193
Glasgow Beasts 2: The Next Incarnation   94
Grail Quest   195
Grammar Lesson   272
Haibun   335
Haibun – To The Deep North   101
Hassan Bids Farewell to his Love   32
Hello My Lovely   175
Hemispheric   336
Home Defence, 1943   71
Home Land   52
Horatian Ode   153
Hotel C'est La Vie   81
Immemoriam   76
In Balladia   141
In which fnc gull begins his homeward flight   131
In which fnc gull deplores slanderous imputations   116
In which fnc gull discourses on sausages and football   120
In which fnc gull makes his will and says his last goodbyes   137
In which fnc gull meditates on devolution and fraternal harmony   118
In which fnc gull meditates on mortality, religion and beaches   133
In which fnc gull offers a critique of conspicuous consumption   129
In which fnc gull returns with tales of travel   125
In which our hero bids farewell (with a hint of later return)   122
In which our hero introduces himself in all his raucous egotism   114
In which our hero meets a formidable mademoiselle   127

In which our radical hero stands out against feudal oppression 135
Ingratitude 228
Insular Poems **265**
Intelligent Design 105
Interview with H.M. 226
Introduction 246
Island Haiku 257
King Robert IV 238
La Mer 39
La Pasión de Don Roberto 235
Lady Gray 309
Las Cabras *(The Goats)* 159
Laughing at Confucius **323**
Legend for Sisyphus Stone 164
LMS Inverness-Kyle, 1942. 268
LOBEY DOSSER RYDZ AGEN 314
Lochar Moss, Summer 1957 293
Lord of the Dance 157
Losing Face 183
Lost Darlings 28
Love Sonnet LXV 61
Love Sonnet LXXII 62
Love Sonnet XI 58
Love Sonnet XVI 59
Love Sonnet XVIII 60
Lunar Eclipse 20
Lykewake Express 310
Maighstir Norman 148
Meetin in the Mist 237
Miracle 57
Mirror Image 227
Miscalculation 67
Mitchell in Mesopotamia 31
Moffat Road, 1941-43 276
Moffat Road, 1943 278
Moffat Road, 1943-46 279

Monarchs of the Glen 199
More from the Pictish Phrase-book 194
Morganstern 146
Mother 74
Muckin Oot the Auld Hame. 208
Nevers 29
New Purchase 82
Night on the Prairie 53
Night-Town 6
Nissen Hut 280
Not the Real Thing 35
October 51
On the Banks of Nith (A Dumfries Youth, 1937-60) 273
On the Buses, Summer 1953, 1954 292
On the Royal Road 324
On the Wireless 186
Once Upon a Time in Orcadia 180
Only a game 328
Other Scots Poems 307
Passing Places 75
Perfect Image 206
Picnic 72
Pictures in an Exhibition 78
Planetary Response 108
Polite Request 89
Politics 33
Poppies No More 337
POTUS Moment 188
President Graham Speaks to the Nation 243
Prewar 266
Primary Sources 225
Prologue: Jeantown 247
Purple I 42
Purple II 43
Queen of Scots 47
R.B. Cunninghame Graham at Glen Aray 240

Rationalisation	87
Recording for Eddie	145
"Rednose", 1947-53	287
Redomones	**139**
Reforestation	50
Reid	19
Remembering Jimmy	154
Returned Exile	270
Returning to Lanark	143
Riding to Trapalanda	**233**
Rood Fair, 1952	289
Rosemount Street, 1960	295
Royal Wedding	204
Saga City	313
Scotia's Hero	30
Sheep in Harris	151
Signs of the Day	24
Skipping Chant	219
Small Stage	107
Social Education Period	202
Sonnet	17
Sonnet on the Departed	326
Sonnet: On Westminster Bridge, 2017	325
Sonnets to Hugh MacDiarmid	**298**
Sorry, Chaps	197
Spectral Desires	63
St Andrew's Day	37
Staff Sonnets	281
Statues	88
Stendhal on a Spanish Balcony	339
Stone Poem	163
Stop the Press	222
Strangers within our Gates	286
Suicide	73
Symposium in the Park with George	201
Tensions	66

The Arrival of the World.   284
The Ballad of Archie McGaw   316
The Bonnie Hind   49
The Broch of Glass   140
The Communication   181
The Falling Apartness of Things   111
The Human Chain – 11/09/13   229
The Interlude   26
The Irruption of Topsy   189
The Last Stories of Kilgore Trout   92
The Nth Dr Who   80
The Numerous Conjunction   214
The Olympians   36
the opinions and emissions of fnc gull, larus argentatus   114
The Owl and the Pussycat   18
The Passion of Don Roberto   234
The Picture of Doreen Gray   79
The Question   223
The Rake   84
The Right Hon. PM Speaks   220
The Right One   86
the saga of fnc gull   113
The Scottish Patient   315
The Sea, The Sea   211
The Seer of Achnashellach Contemplates Religion   191
The Selkie and the Drunks   9
The Sleep of Reason   221
the travels and further effusions of fnc gull vagabond extraordinaire   124
The Verdict   231
The Who   212
These Times   55
Thieves of Baghdad   40
Torridons   14
Touché, Touché!   327
Trapalanda   236
Tripli City   70

Turn of the Season   165
Two Views   224
Uniforms   16
View from the Gallery Wall   171
View from the Island   269
Vision   166
Walking to the Island   **245**
Watershed   215
Welcome   200
What the Ancients Did for Us —The Picts   190
Where Have You Sprung From?   77
Whit's in a Name?   322
Writing   216

Biographical Note

Alan MacGillivray is of Highland parentage but was brought up in Dumfries in the South-West of Scotland. For many years he taught English in schools in Annan, Inverness and Lerwick, and in Jordanhill College and Strathclyde University in Glasgow. He has written and published extensively on Scottish literary topics and is a Past President and Honorary Fellow of the Association for Scottish Literature. Since 2005 he has produced eight poetry collections, which include many poems in varieties of Scots, several of which have been prize-winners in the annual James McCash Scots Poetry Competition.